Soaring Seniors

Stories,
Steps & Strategies
for Living Full-Out after Fifty,
Sixty, Seventy...

Rita Losee, ScD, RN

authorHOUSE®

AuthorHouse™
1663 Liberty Drive
Bloomington, IN 47403
www.authorhouse.com
Phone: 1 (800) 839-8640

Published by AuthorHouse 12/28/2018

ISBN: 978-1-5462-7368-4 (sc)
ISBN: 978-1-5462-7369-1 (hc)
ISBN: 978-1-5462-7367-7 (e)

Library of Congress Control Number: 2018915057

Print information available on the last page.

Any people depicted in stock imagery provided by Getty Images are models,
and such images are being used for illustrative purposes only.
Certain stock imagery © Getty Images.

This book is printed on acid-free paper.

Because of the dynamic nature of the Internet, any web addresses or links contained in
this book may have changed since publication and may no longer be valid. The views
expressed in this work are solely those of the author and do not necessarily reflect the
views of the publisher, and the publisher hereby disclaims any responsibility for them.

Book design: Guernsey Graphics
Cover photo: Andrew Estey
soaringseniors.com
facebook.com/Soaring-Seniors-Unlimited-241602776553973/

This book offers health, fitness and nutritional information and is designed for educational
purposes only. You should not rely on this information as a substitute for, nor does it replace,
professional medical advice, diagnosis, or treatment. Nor is it intended as a substitute
for advice and recommendations of your financial advisors, personal tax expert, or legal
advisers. Suggestions included in this book should be followed only after consulting with
one's personal physicians and other professionals. The author/publisher expressly disclaim
responsibility for any adverse effects from the information contained within this book.

RAVES FOR *SOARING SENIORS*

"Rita, your book is GREAT! Love the energy, insights, tips. There is a real exuberance in your book that brings new life in the reader — and me! Well done."

~ Joe Vitale, author of *Zero Limits*

"Rita H. Losee has put together a beautifully, clearly written, practical, person-friendly, and comprehensive approach for anyone over age 50. Soaring Seniors empowers each of us take action steps to gain muscle, energy, vitality, and mobility no matter what age. You will call it informative, educational, and actionable and I call it in Rita's language 'inspirACTional'."

~ Anne M. Moreau RNC, BSN Nutritionist/Health Coach
    Proactive Health With Anne, LLC

"I love the name of this book. Just saying 'Soaring Seniors' I can feel a vibrational lift and as we know the higher the vibration the better our results. You'll find in here so many useful tips for keeping a high vibration that it's one of those books you'll want to have nearby at all times. Rita is an authority on what can go wrong if you don't have the right information about keeping soaring."

~ Ros Goldsborough, Unity Prosperity Facilitator

"Soaring Seniors is practical, entertaining and fun! Rita Losee shared powerful 21 Tips that will inspire you and transform you to creating new levels of health, wealth, and happiness as a senior, no matter your age."

~ David Riklan, founder of Self-Growth.com

"I have read your book and it's a really fun read, full of great advice and very relatable examples. I appreciate that it has information for the novice and those already well versed in health and nutrition."

~ Rebecca Beauchamp

"Rita Losee is an inspirational woman. Having the courage to fight through extreme physical adversity she had been able to discover secrets to vitality, wellness and recovery in her later life that few people ever learn. Rita put herself in a position to transform her life because of her courage and willingness to take risks and go for her dreams. I highly recommend that you pay attention to the secrets of Rita's journey and see if you can discover the power of her lessons learned."
~ David Raynr, Transformational facilitator & speaker

"Soaring Seniors soars! Rita Losee has brought an invaluable resource to print. These make-life-wonderful [tips] will help inspire anyone to live life to the fullest, at every age. Rita's fun side fills every page— from plentiful, optimistic word plays right down to the engaging format of this winning book."
~ Nola Fennessy, Entrepreneur

"Rita Losee provides an authentic and easy to read guide for improving quality of life at any age. She is an inspiration, and someone I have always respected and admired. I especially like the step-by-step approach, in which the benefits that you gain from step one will motivate you to move to step two and beyond."
~ Stephen Cherniske, author of *The DHEA Breakthrough*

"In Soaring Seniors, Rita has captured practical approaches to better health and quality of life for any age...not just seniors! Health, or lack thereof, is in a crisis mode in many countries; with obesity, diabetes, opioids, and today's sedentary lifestyle, many suffer and are in great need of these tips. Soaring Seniors offers a practical guide to bridging from your current state to a better quality of life."
~ Dr. R. L. R. Bietz: PhD-MBA-MS-BS.ChE-Diploma
  Personal & Legacy Mentor to Her Majesty Queen Elizabeth II: Queen's Young Leaders
  Founder & CEO: BioRev, LLC
  President of the Board of Directors: Serve First (501c3)
  President of Univera, Inc. (USA, Canada, Mexico, & Mexico Holding Ltd.)

"What I love about Soaring Seniors is the message of hope it gives to everyone over 50, 60, 70 and up. Rita Losee's natural wit and way with words along with her knowledge of how the human body works make this book extremely 'edu-taining'. Whether you are in the same decade as Rita or not, you'll get a firm feel for the verve with which she wants everyone to live. Read the book, pick a tip and start your journey to joyful, healthy living with Rita as your fun-loving guide. This is a great book!"

~ Tam Veilleux, creator of *The Magic Maker's Planner + Playbook*
choosebigchange.com

"Rita Losee is a gift for anyone who wants to live a fuller life! She is a role model for what is possible for us as we get older! Her book is fantastic! Read it and learn from Rita's wisdom!"

~ Eric Lofholm, Sales Champion, Founder of Paradise Adopt a Family

"Soaring Seniors has a wealth of information for all ages, not just over-the-age-of-65 seniors. However, as a senior herself, Rita reminds the rest of us seniors that this particular age delineation for "retirement" stems from the 19th century! Rita tells us that we have certainly progressed a few centuries beyond into the 21st century. We can most definitely live a vibrant life for decades past age 65 if we play our "life cards" more effectively. Thank you, Rita, for this reminder to use her stories, steps and strategies to improve the quality of our 21st century senior life."

~ Catheryne Draper, 21st century senior and author of *Winning the Math Homework Challenge, User-Friendly Math for Parents, How the Math Gets Done,* and *Spatial Sense Makes Math Sense*

"Rita Losee offers individuals practical coaching advice and useful strategies so a person can live their best senior years with passion. Her book is filled with stories that inspire a person to take action for living a happier, healthier, and wealthier life, while remaining an empowered participant in today's world."

~Dhebi DeWitz, author of *The Messenger Within: Unlocking the Secrets to Greater Freedom and a Better Life.*

Show-Stopping, Jaw-Dropping, Startling Statistics

OVERWEIGHT/OBESITY/DIABETES

In 2015, there were 1.6 million deaths worldwide directly caused by diabetes.

medscape.org/viewarticle/902631?nlid=126088_2713&src=wnl_cmemp_181116_mscpedu_nurs&uac=269465SY&impID=1800781&faf=1

Diabetes and prediabetes affect 73% of older Americans.

AARP: The Magazine. April/May 2018. P 36

The American Diabetes Association released new research on March 22, 2018 estimating the total costs of diagnosed diabetes have risen to $327 billion in 2017 from $245 billion in 2012, when the cost was last examined.

diabetes.org/advocacy/news-events/cost-of-diabetes.html

Eighty-seven- and one-half percent of adults are overweight or obese.

diabetes.org/assets/pdfs/basics/cdc-statistics-report-2017.pdf

Cost of obesity: $147 billion annually (in 2008 dollars).

cdc.gov/obesity/adult/causes.html

There are 2.1 BILLION people on the planet who are overweight or obese.

healthdata.org/news-release/nearly-one-third-world%E2%80%99s-population-obese-or-overweight-new-data-show

Eighty percent of obese people are metabolically disordered.

Wachter, Robert. *The Digital Doctor: Hope, Hype, and Harm at the Dawn of the Medicine's Computer Age.* New York: McGraw Hill. 2015. P 16

"Sugar is the other white powder." (P 5) [1]

"Sugared beverages cause 180,000 deaths per year worldwide." (P 270) [1]

[1]Lustig, Robert. *The Hacking of the American Mind: The Science Behind the Corporate Takeover of Our Bodies and Brains.* New York: Avery. 2017

STATINS

...with at least *300 adverse health effects* evident in the published literature so far, with at least 28 distinct modes of toxicity, including:

- Muscle damage (myotoxicity): 80 studies
- Nerve damage (neurotoxicity): 54 studies
- Liver damage (hepatoxocity): 32 studies
- Endocrine disruption: 16 studies
- Cancer-promoting: 9 studies
- Diabetes-promoting: 8 studies
- Cardiovascular-damaging: 15 studies
- Birth defect causing (teratogenic): 11 studies

kellybroganmd.com/cracking-cholesterol-myth-statins-harm-body-mind/

Statin prescriptions increased 80% from 2002 to 2013.

uspharmacist.com/article/use-of-statins-way-up-but-costs-have-dropped

Spending on cholesterol drugs in the United States alone reached nearly $19 billion in 2010.

articles.mercola.com/sites/articles/archive/2012/02/01/
29-billion-reasons-to-lie-about-cholesterol.aspx

Total sales for statins are expected to reach $1 trillion (U.S.) by 2020. Lipitor is the most profitable drug in medical history.

michaelwest.com.au/statin-wars-secrecy-and-the-worlds-most-lucrative-drugs/

DEATH, DISEASE, DOCTORS & DRUGS

One-third of Americans die before age 65. Only half live to age 78.

Flanigan,MD, Richard & Flanigan Sawyer, MD, Kate. *Longevity Made Simple: How to Add 20 Good Years to Your Life.* Denver, CO: Williams Clark Publishing. 2007. P 3

The average couple retiring today at age 65 will need $280,000 to cover health care and medical costs in retirement (on original Medicare).

time.com/money/5246882/heres-how-much-the-average-couple-will-spend-on-health-care-costs-in-retirement/Apr 19, 2018

...a couple retiring today will spend 67% of their Social Security benefits on health care costs over their lifetimes.
For a couple retiring in 10 years (2025) at age 65, medical care will suck up 90% of their Social Security income.

time.com/money/3758785/health-care-costs-retirement/ (dated 2015)

One in ten Americans 65 and older has been diagnosed with Alzheimer's.

AARP Bulletin, October/November, 2018. P 42

Ten percent of all U.S. deaths are now due to medical error, totaling more than 250,000 deaths per year.

hopkinsmedicine.org/news/media/releases/study_suggests_medical_errors_now_third_leading_cause_of_death_in_the_us, May 2106

Eighty percent of the active ingredients in U.S. medicines come from China and India. (P 37) [2]

China controls more than 60 percent of the world supply of vitamin C. (P 69) [2]

[2]Gibson, Rosemary. *China Rx: Exposing the Risks of America's Dependence on China for Medicine.* Amherst, NY: Prometheus Books. 2018.

Individuals aged 50 years or older accounted for 70% of dispensed prescriptions in 2016 (a script for 84 or more days counted as three).

medscape.com/viewarticle/879514?nlid=114644_2822&src=WNL_mdplsnews_170505_mscpedit_nurs&uac=269465SY&spon=24&impID=1341995&faf=1

...up to 90 percent of all known human illnesses
can be traced back to an unhealthy gut.

Perlmutter, MD, David. *Brain Maker: The Power of Gut Microbes to Heal
and Protect Your Brain — for Life.* New York: Little Brown & Company. 2015.

"Today, the average elderly patient in the United States
sees seven physicians (two generalists and five specialists)
in four different practices each year."

Wachter, Robert. *The Digital Doctor: Hope, Hype, and Harm at the Dawn
of the Medicine's Computer Age.* New York: McGraw Hill. 2015. P 43

Prescription drugs caused almost 1.3 million
emergency room visits and 124, 000 deaths in 2014.

Consumer Reports, September, 2017

Seventy-five to ninety percent of patients do NOT receive
adequate warnings about drug side effects. (P 5) [3]

Drug companies have spent billions to convince doctors that
clinical trials are the only worthwhile form of medical proof. (P 82) [3]

[3]Cohen, MD, Jay S. *What You Must Know about the Hidden Dangers of Antibiotics:
How the Side Effects of Six Popular Antibiotics Can Destroy Your Health.*
Garden City Park, New York: Square One Publishers. 2018.

Almost 75 percent of adults had systolic blood pressure of
140 mm Hg or higher or diastolic blood pressure of
90 mm Hg or higher, or they were on prescription medication
for high blood pressure.

diabetes.org/assets/pdfs/basics/cdc-statistics-report-2017.pdf

Medical doctors live about ten years less than others.

Collins, MD, Kathryn. *How Healthy is Your doctor? What Your Doctor
Doesn't Know about Health Could be Hazardous to Yours.*
Teton Village, WY: Whitegrass Press. 2013. P 1

"All-cause mortality is decreased by about 30% to 35% in
physically active, as compared to inactive subjects."

ncbi.nlm.nih.gov/pmc/articles/PMC3395188/

"In the first six months of the Trump administration, the pharmaceutical industry spent $145 million on lobbying." (P 108) [4]

"There is a group of doctors whose specialty is pain relief, sponsored by opioid manufacturers whose goal is to block restrictions on painkiller prescriptions." (P 131) [4]

"By 2016, eight of the nine major drug makers had paid billions of dollars over the prior decade for violating a criminal statute prohibiting what is called off-label marketing — promoting drugs for uses not approved by the FDA." (P 288) [4]

[4]Brill, Steven. *Tailspin: The People and Forces Behind America's Fifty-Year Fall — and Those fighting to Reverse It.* New York. Alfred A. Knopf. 2018.

Up to 50% of folks in their seventies have insomnia. (P 36) [5]

Twenty percent of women have osteoporosis by age 80. (P 41) [5]

Almost twenty percent of men and 25% of women have chronic foot pain. (P 40) [5]

[5]*AARP: The Magazine.* April/May 2018

DIET AND EXERCISE

Three percent! The number of people who 1) don't smoke, 2) eat a nutritious diet, 3), exercise regularly, and 4) maintain healthy weight.

Flanigan, MD, Richard & Flanigan Sawyer, MD, Kate. *Longevity Made Simple: How to Add 20 Good Years to Your Life.* Denver, CO: Williams Clark Publishing. 2007. P xiii

Every year in the U.S. consumers spend at least *$12.8 billion on natural health supplements.*

Hansen, Carolyn. Email accessed 11/15/18.

In 2012, 6 million of the 43 million Americans sixty-five
or older needed daily help with ADLs (Activities of Daily Living)
such as bathing, preparing food.

diabetes.org/assets/pdfs/basics/cdc-statistics-report-2017.pdf

Eating nuts can "reduce heart attack risk by 30 percent." (P 11)[6]

Curcumin (spice in curry) is anti-inflammatory.
A university study found that memory and attention spans
improved in adults ages 51 – 84, who took 90 mg of curcumin
twice a day for 18 months. (P 16)[6]

[6]*AARP.org/Bulletin*. Vol.59, No.4. May, 2018.

Three hundred thousand Americans are hospitalized
with broken hips; 95% are due to a fall.
Falls are the "leading cause of fatal injury among older adults."

aging.com/falls-fact-sheet/

Every 19 minutes, an older adult dies from a fall.

ncoa.org/news/resources-for-reporters/get-the.../falls-prevention-facts/

In a twenty-year study of the leading causes of death,
the Institute for Health Metrics and Evaluation concluded
diet is "fueling the deaths of tens of millions of people — and
more than 600,000 Americans — every single year."

Ocean Robbins email

"Hundreds of samples of poultry, beef, and pork
appeared to show residue of drugs that the government says
should never be used in food animals (italics mine). (P 32)[7]

Banned drugs found: phenylbutazone (not for human use),
ketamine, (banned because of use as illegal hallucinogenic) and
nitroimidazoles (likely carcinogens). (P 35)[7]

[7]*Consumer Reports*. October, 2018.

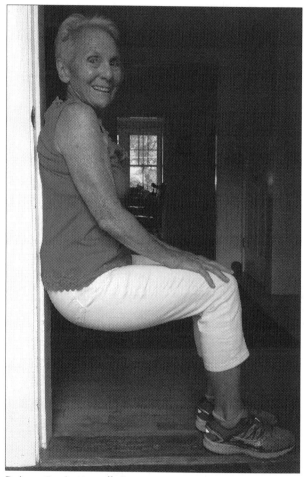

Doing a 5-minute wall sit.

INTRODUCTION
Why Did I Write This Book?

High school graduation! What an exciting time! I sat behind the flood-lights eager and excited to live my life as an adult! Finally! I had waited so long for that day. Graduation day was the first time I completed the experience of being a senior. I didn't know then that I would embrace other senior experiences, always with the joyous expectancy of entering an exciting new phase of my life.

Joyous expectancy, that is, until I became a "senior," where my unconscious (and some not-so-unconscious) expectations and that of my culture, were that I was now entering the stage of 4Ds: diminishment, deterioration, disease and death. This presented an entirely new and not-very-fun attitude about being a senior. That cultural path had no appeal.

In the U.S., the traditional age for retirement is 65. In his book, *The Longevity Economy: Unlocking the World's Fastest-Growing, Most Misunderstood Market,* Joseph Coughlin explains that the Union Army established pensions for Civil War veterans and widows in the 1890s where recipients were eligible in their sixties. He states that by 1900 the program accounted for "almost 30% of the federal budget." Worse, from my perspective, Coughlin goes on to state, "But physicians, who already viewed old age as intrinsically debilitating..." Whoa! As I talk with my peers, it seems that attitude is alive and well in 2018. How many of us have heard doctors dismiss symptoms with, 'You're getting old.'"?

In the U.S. in 1900, the average age of death was 47. In 2015, it was 78.4 years (interesting to note, both English and Japanese have longer life expectancies). As of April, 2010, there were 43 plus million Americans over age 65. Ten thousand baby boomers will turn 65 *every day* for the next eleven years.

finance.yahoo.com/news/10-000-boomers-turn-65-111500689.html

What a huge loss of intellectual power and experience if all those millions and millions of us no longer are actively contributing to the well-being of community and culture. What a huge prosperity deficit we are creating. That is one very big reason for me to write this book!

I am happiness! I am health! I am wealth!

What awful expectations and beliefs underlie the messages, spoken and unspoken, as we expect millions of us to lose — lose our health; lose our earning capacity, lose our productivity; lose our minds; lose our ability to be independent, contributing, and a vital part of our world. One of the reasons I wrote this book is I think there are much healthier, happier, and wealthier expectations/beliefs we can create — for the good of all of us!

I believe that most of my age cohort want to be contributors to the prosperity of the world. I know that I do, another good reason for writing this book. If you are one of the really savvy, or lucky, ones who have adequate retirement money and you are fulfilled by whatever activities you choose, go for it!

If, however, you do not have adequate retirement funds, why not choose to be productive and a participant in the world's economy — and in your own? According to the Economic Policy Institute, a 2013 study found that families between the ages of 56 and 65 had an average of $17,000 in retirement savings. Even with a good Social Security payment, it's quite clear most of us won't be soaring very far or high on that!

The age of retirement we all came to accept was arbitrarily established and became encoded into our expectations. Just because "they" decided we were to be "put out to pasture" at 65, doesn't mean we can't choose another alternative.

Another reason I decided to be a soaring senior and write this book is my background as a nurse and counselor. One of the questions that has fascinated me for my entire life is, "What makes humans think and act the way we do?"

I am happiness! I am health! I am wealth!

We have two minds, our conscious mind and our unconscious mind. (Of course, that separatist split is one that we've created with our human minds. Our minds are not divided into pieces like Legos. We conceptualize them as conscious and unconscious in order to facilitate our understanding, but they are one intricately connected operating system.) Of the two, the unconscious is much more powerful and tends to drive our behaviors. Our beliefs about what being a senior citizen, being old, would be like got laid down decades ago when we were very young; those expectations were implanted into our brains and psyches by our parents, grandparents, schools, and religious organizations before we were seven years old. Indeed, some of those beliefs have been part of our heritage for generations.

As little kids, we have no filter to understand and analyze whether what we are being told by the adults around us is true or not. We are not able to think about what Mom or Dad or other role models say makes sense or not. No little kid ever thinks, when Mom or Dad makes a statement, "Gee, what she's saying really doesn't add up. Don't think she's right about that one."

We just suck it all in to our fledgling selves and take it as gospel truth.

Think about your grandparents. What did they think? How did they act? Were they robustly healthy? Were they exercising every day? Consciously eating for health? Did they have joyous aspirations for their futures? Did they talk with you about how exciting their lives were and how much fun they were having? Earning money and expecting to earn more in the future? How delighted they were with their lives? Their goals and aspirations? Probably not!

Our brains think in images. Those early images of the older people who were part of our lives got encoded in our brains and bodies (Even though we tend to think of brains and bodies as separate, they are NOT!). Those beliefs form the basic images of being older. If we believe it, it will be our reality.

Think about it, haven't you always expected that when you are over 65, you'll have gray hair (or very little), wrinkles on your face, and sagging sections all over your body?

I am happiness! I am health! I am wealth!

I have four awesome grandchildren. I am endeavoring to give them a much more active, involved, and robust image of being older. As a graduate student, I learned that we have three sources of learning: didactic, role modeling, and experiential. In the course of this book, I am going to encourage you to use all three. Didactic: you will find facts, new information and ideas here, just as you did as a student in school. Role modeling: it is my hope that you will see pictures in here and think, "If she can do that, wonder what I can do?"

Experiential? In January, 2010, I was musing about New Year's resolutions and came to the conclusion that we all want the results we typically name, such as those perennial favorites — getting fitter, losing weight and saving more money. What we don't want to do is actually make the changes and do the work required to get those results. Consequently, the next year arrives and we simply recycle last year's resolutions.

I decided in January, 2016 that for the rest of my life, I would set the same New Year's Intention: once a month, I would do something *I had never done before, ever,* just for fun. I love that intention and I love the experiences and memories I now have.

Welcome to a world of new and fun experiences! Welcome to the growing world of Soaring Seniors!

"You can't help getting older, but you do not have to get old."

– GEORGE BURNS

STEP #1
Move! Frequently and Often

STORY

In my very early thirties, I was a young mother of the cutest little boy. One gorgeous summer afternoon I put him down for a nap and retreated to my porch with a book. I read, **"Life is either a daring adventure or nothing at all."** Those ten words changed my life irrevocably.

I instantly decided to live a life of adventure. As I now view that experience, it was inspired and I took action. My commitment to a life of adventure began — consciously — that summer afternoon.

But, I was the woman who within months of becoming an RN had convinced my roommate to quit our jobs and spend three months traveling across the United States in her '62 Chevy Impala. I was already acting as a woman of adventure, I just wasn't conscious of it.

Shortly after being jolted by Helen Keller's words, I wrote the mission statement of my life: *My life is to be a life of adventure. During the course of my adventure, I intend to master all that I can, physically, intellectually, emotionally and spiritually and share what I learn with as many people as I can.*

I haven't changed a word of my mission statement in the forty-five plus years since I wrote it. It has served me magnificently well. Whenever I encounter a major decision and I'm unsure of which direction to go, I simply ask myself, "Rita, what would a woman of adventure do here?" I inevitably get instant clarity about the "right" answer to my question.

I am happiness! I am health! I am wealth!

This book begins with a step to move more; it is particularly valuable for seniors or wannabe seniors to move more. Sometimes the movement is physical movement. Sometimes it is about moving intellectually or emotionally or spiritually. Life is always about moving!

Your body was designed to move. A major distinguishing characteristic of dead people is that they are not moving. If you want to be more lifelike and lively, get in motion.

As a kid, I played outdoors — a lot. That was what kids of my generation did. I swam, climbed trees, jumped out of the hay mow, went sliding and ice skating. In addition, I walked ¾ of a mile every morning to catch the school bus. That laid the base for a lifetime of being physically active. I also heard stories of my maternal grandfather riding his bicycle in 1913 from Orono, Maine to West Bath, Maine. He didn't have a ten-speed, roads weren't paved, and family legend is that he arrived on a hot June day and rode directly into the cove.

I have in my family archives a newspaper photo showing my maternal grandmother on the high school basketball team in 1906! It was a very long time before I realized that the girl was out there for that time. Interestingly, the uniform she and her teammates wore looked a whole lot like the one I wore when I went to that high school decades later.

I am happiness! I am health! I am wealth!

Can you Law of Attraction fans see the links I see between my maternal grandparents (my grandmother died long before I was born) and my own passion for being physically active? I certainly can.

In my early thirties I became a runner. Because of George Banks' influence, I started running in the very early seventies, before the invention of running shoes; the only other folks I saw running were those weird men training for marathons. Certainly, I didn't encounter other women when I first started running.

I ran for decades, in all kinds of weather, no matter what else was going on in my life. Running was a priority. Then, after a major metabolic meltdown in January, 2010, I was forced to endure years without being able to run. There were days when my "exercise" was reduced to being able to walk for five minutes, max, before my metabolism virtually flat-lined and I was forced back to the couch to recover from the exertion.

In all those couch slouch years, I never stopped being a runner in my mind and heart. Now in my mid-seventies, I am once again a runner. Last year, on virtually no training, I took first place in a 5k in the over-sixty women group; it was several years ago that I was chronologically sixty.

What I now realize is that all the running and other intense physical activities I did for decades were making deposits in my fitness bank; by the time I got ill I had a huge compilation of deposits to draw on.

As I've recovered, I have been astounded at how quickly my exercise capacity has been restored. Simultaneously, I've discovered how challenging it can be to get an unfit body and mind to re-establish the habit. I still struggle to get my exercise back to the level I would really love.

I am happiness! I am health! I am wealth!

"A body in motion tends to stay in motion" applies to physical bodies, too. It takes more mental energy and determination to get a habit incorporated into one's life than it does to keep a well-established habit going.

What does exercise/moving your body do for you?

1. Improves circulation in every cell in your body. Every cell in your body needs oxygen and nutrients; those are delivered via your blood stream. Exercise keeps your blood streaming.

2. Builds/keeps muscle.
   - Muscle is metabolically active tissue that needs more energy than fat.
   - Muscle is more compact than fat. If you want to look good in your genes/jeans, you want more muscle.
   - A pound of muscle added to your body will require 50 calories a day.
   - "Sitting is the new smoking." Huffington Post Blog title
   huffingtonpost.com/the-active-times/sitting-is-the-new-smokin_b_5890006.html

3. Gives you more energy. Energy in your body is created by mitochondria, organelles in the nuclei of your cells. The more mitochondria your cells have, the more energy your body can produce. Exercise builds mitochondria.

4. Helps you sleep better.

5. Relieves stress. According to Mark Hyman, MD, over 90% of contemporary disease is stress-related.

6. Creates a look you love in your mirror.

7. Boosts your immune system.

8. *I am happiness! I am health! I am wealth!*

9. Helps stave off the cognitive decline that is almost expected as we age. Don't fall for that expectation trap! Cognitive decline may be "normal" in westernized countries, but it certainly isn't desirable.

10. Improves your mood. Exercise has been proven to be an effective treatment for depression, more so than prescribed antidepressants for mild to moderate depression. Unlike prescription drugs, the side effect of exercise is better health!

11. Provides a good excuse to get outdoors. For eons, humans lived in the outdoors; only in the past few generations have we almost totally separated ourselves from Mother Nature. There is research evidence that "forest bathing," hanging out with trees, is health inducing.

    I deliberately live in a camper during the summer in a most idyllic spot on the coast of Maine. I am on the deck with my morning coffee before sunrise most mornings. I often work on the deck; I get inordinate pleasure from being outside. I also get a health bonus.

12. Builds BDNF, *brain-derived neutrogenic factor*. If you've not ever been introduced to BDNF before, it is my pleasure! BDNF not only helps you grow new brain cells, it helps you keep the ones you have in tip top shape.

More about BDNF: people with Parkinson's, Alzheimer's, and perhaps depression have less. Higher levels enhance memory, mood, and executive functioning and it is "a powerful promoter of brain plasticity in the long term." (*Genius Foods*, p 42)

13. Enables you to eat more without gaining weight. I love this one; eating is one of my favorite indoor sports.

14. Helps you stay "regular."

15. Helps you keep strong bones. Hip fractures start a death spiral for thousands of seniors every year.

16. Enables you to enjoy more frequent sex. (Think seniors don't think about sex? Or have sex?)

17. Reduces insulin resistance; in a country where type 2 diabetes affects almost 50% of the adult population, this is critical.

    Insulin resistance occurs when your cells have a diminished capacity to utilize insulin; thus, prompting your pancreas to make more. When your pancreas can no longer keep up with the demand, it poops out and you have diabetes. Once you are diabetic, your body is in a rapidly descending downward spiral.

18. Helps keep your blood pressure in a healthy range. In a country where 33 percent of the adult U.S. population has high blood pressure, this is a very good thing. (American Heart Association)

19. Reduces inflammation. Please note the root of the word, "inflammation" is in-flames. Not good for either your house or your cells.

20. Helps prevent cardiovascular disease.

21. Can increase pain tolerance and/or reduce the perception of pain.

22. Creates endorphins, the body's built in morphine. Exercise high is real and beneficial. Manmade opiates kill!

23. Can help reduce your health care costs.

nytimes.com/2016/09/07/well/move/whats-the-value-of-exercise-2500.html

This article indicated that exercisers can save $2500 annually. Obese people, male or female, consistently get paid less; that was true 30 years ago when I was reviewing literature for my dissertation. It's still true today. I am certainly spending less on health care now, way less than I was in my couch slouch years.

24. Can boost your self-esteem and reduce anxiety.

25. Increases lung capacity.

Question: If I had a pill that would give you all those benefits, what would you pay me?

Answer: *Anything I asked.*

STRATEGIES

1. Because it is a challenge to get an exercise habit established, particularly if you are a senior, it's is ever so helpful to join a class. Putting some cash on the barrel increases the likelihood you'll actually show up. Find a fitness facility close to home/work. That also increases the likelihood when class starts, you'll be there. You'll also develop friendships, giving you another boost of motivation. Ditto, for engaging a friend as an exercise buddy.

2. If you are over age 50, it is a good idea to get your DHEA sulfate level done (the blood test is DHEA-s). DHEA is an adrenal hormone we all produce a lot of as young adults, but less and less as decades go by. Low DHEA levels can make exercise very uncomfortable and unrewarding for older folks. Our bodies need DHEA in order for cells to heal. (More about DHEA later.)

3. Vary your activity. Just as our bodies experience weight loss plateaus, we will create exercise plateaus if we keep doing the same routine, week in, week out.

After a morning spent primarily at my computer, my body, especially my butt, started demanding that I get up and move. I love being outdoors, so decided to go for a walk. I walked my accustomed route, flat, certainly not challenging. I found a chunk of ice and started kicking it along in front of me, using both feet. (No, not at the same time!) Suddenly, my walk got a whole lot more interesting and fun.

Did I get a huge muscular benefit from the changed activity? No, but I got some. AND, I greatly increased the fun factor.

4. *I am happiness! I am health! I am wealth!*

5. Give yourself permission to start VERY slowly if you've been sedentary for a long time.

6. Work out early in the day. That shifts it from your to-do list to your TAH-DAH list, setting you up for healthier behaviors for the rest of the day.

7. Housebound? Unable to walk? Have limited mobility? Do whatever you can to move whatever you can move more often. You have the rest of your life to keep improving your capacity.

8. Here are some fascinating research results I found in Joe Dispenza's newest book, *Becoming Supernatural*. Researchers put casts on the healthy wrists of 29 volunteers, with half practicing imagining exercising their arms for 11 minutes a day, five days/week for one month. The other half of the group did nothing. At the end of the month, those who mentally practiced strengthening their muscles had muscles that were twice as strong as those who did nothing. That, and several other studies I've known about for years, tells me that even if we can't move a muscle, imagining moving it will build its capacity! What great news!

9. Use it or lose it rules! If you're over fifty, you'll lose it faster than when you were in your thirties. That doesn't matter. You can gain it back!

10. Don't like to exercise? First, see Step #7. There are reversible physiological reasons why that may be the case for you.

11. Don't call it exercise. Saying "I have to exercise," has the appeal of wearing a hair shirt and you'll perceive activity as punishment. Reframe the concept into, "I'm going out to play."

12. Actually, refrain from ever saying, "I have to," or "I can't." Those statements mean you are giving your power and control to something outside of you.

I am happiness! I am health! I am wealth!

Rock climbing in New Hampshire.

"The doctor of the future will give no medicine, but instead will interest his patients in the care of the human frame, in diet, and in the cause and prevention of disease."

– THOMAS EDISON

STEP #2
Develop Diversity of Movement

A STORY

Many years ago, George said, "Rita, you ought to start running." Because I had grown up being physically active, with family role models who were also, and because I loved physical activity, it was fairly easy for me to think running was a good idea.

I started running... then life would interfere and my running would taper to a halt. Then, George would ask, "How's the running going?" Ooops! His reminders served as a prod; I'd start running again.

It took one full year of fits and starts with him providing gentle prods before running was my habit, sustainable from the inside. Now, after years of enforced sedentariness, I am once again back in the fits and starts period of re-establishing my running habit.

I am happiness! I am health! I am wealth!

Wherever you are on your fitness journey, keep moving, moving toward the goal of being more fit tomorrow than you are today.

There are three types of exercise to build into your life: aerobic, anaerobic (aka weights), and stretching. First, let's talk about aerobic, which literally means "with oxygen".

Aerobic

Running, walking, rowing, biking, elliptical machines, climbing stairs, and gardening all qualify as aerobic. You want to get your pulse rate up and keep it up. A good rule of thumb is to move fast enough so your breathing increases but you can still talk without gasping for breath.

When you are breathing hard, you are moving aerobically. How much aerobic exercise should you get? The Mayo Clinic recommends 150 minutes of moderate aerobic exercise per week. That sounds like a lot of time invested, but it's only 20 minutes a day! More and more sources conclude that dividing the 20 minutes into two separate sessions works just as well.

I am happiness! I am health! I am wealth!

Move the intensity up to vigorous, and 75 minutes a week will meet your minimum weekly requirement for aerobic exercise. As you progress — and you will — consider adding high intensity interval training aka HIIT. To do HIITs, simply pick up the pace of what you are doing to the really hard gasping level for 30 seconds or so, then slow your pace to a comfortable level. Two or three HIITs during a workout will leave you soaring and ever so proud of yourself. And more fit!

Weights

Lifting weights, whether you are lifting barbells, milk bottles filled with sand, or using your body as the weight, as in squats and planks, is the second essential piece of your exercise strategy. Those are the exercises that are building muscle on your body. You want every single muscle cell on your body that you can have!

I am happiness! I am health! I am wealth!

One of the most noticeable signs of approaching death is muscle wasting, known in the medical world as "myopenia or "sarcopenia'." As my mother deteriorated over the last several months of her life, she became skin and bones, a state I referred to as "frailing." Frailing is NOT healthy!

If you are a woman and are concerned about looking like Arnold Schwarzenegger in his prime, worry not. As a woman your hormones will keep you from getting that bulky.

Decades ago, I came across research that was published by Wayne Wescott who worked at Boston South Shore YMCA. He was training folks over 90 to work with weights; they were increasing muscle mass.

Nice to know you are never too old to build muscle. Muscle is good to own! A nice side benefit, muscles are sexy.

Stretching

The third type of exercise we should all be doing is stretching. Think of an old elastic band that has oxidized, dried out and lost its stretch ability. It's lost its power and can't perform its function. Your muscles will tend to tighten over time. If you don't stretch them, they, too, will lose power and function. If you don't believe me, jump up right now, and attempt to touch your toes. Carefully! Your back muscles may be desperately in need of stretching!

I am happiness! I am health! I am wealth!

If your immediate reaction to my request was, "I can't. I have a bad back," I'll bet those muscles have tightened and lost their elasticity. So, make sure you stretch, gently and carefully.

If you are thinking, I don't have time to do all that exercise, check this out:

In a study by the National Institute of Health, researchers examined the longevity gains made by adults 40 years or older, with varying exercise regimes. Keeping in mind other factors that could impact life expectancy, such as socioeconomic status, the study found that doing the recommended 150 minutes of moderate exercise (or 75 minutes of vigorous exercise) per week added approximately 3.4 extra years to one's life. Doing twice the recommended dose meant an additional 4.2 years to one's life. Even doing half the recommended amount made for gains of 1.8 years. Therefore, according to the researchers' calculations, you gain seven extra minutes of life for every minute of exercise. As Tom Anthony, a Harvard University graduate who assisted in these calculations, said, "I wish I could get these paybacks in the stock market".
nytimes.com/2016/09/07/well/move/whats-the-value-of-exercise-2500.html

I am happiness! I am health! I am wealth!

I'll happily take an extra three to four healthy years of life on this planet. Another thought, science has discovered that the human body has a capacity for at least 120 healthy years. We live in a very exciting time of growth of the health sciences. If there is a breakthrough that could really give me the opportunity to extend my productive years for several more decades, I'm there!

I also recognize that many of my age cohort do not make that choice. I doubt that many of them have picked up this book to read. Unfortunately, those folks are the ones who need it most.

If you haven't exercised for a long period of time, please see your medical practitioner (preferably one who exercises herself) and get baseline assessment and guidance. Do what you can to establish safe guidelines. It's also a good idea to get a personal trainer or work out with a certified fitness professional.

STRATEGIES

1. Yoga. Yoga gives one strengthening, balance practice (very often balance is a challenge for seniors), stretching, and stress release. My newest passion is aerial yoga. It is so much fun and hanging upside down creates a rush of blood flow to the brain. Blood flow to, and through, one's brain is a good thing!

2. If you watch 30 minutes of television per day, you have time for exercise. Walk in place, lift weights, or do yoga while the news is on. Even just exercising during the commercials will pay off handsomely over time.

3. Hit the mute button during the commercials and skip the brainwashing of the drug commercials.

4. It is beyond the scope of this book to suggest specific exercises to do and how to do them. There are an enormous number of resources for that. A great place to start is your local Y. Get information about Silver Sneakers, exercise activities designed especially for seniors.

5. If you really loathe exercise and try to force yourself to do it, you'll likely quit at the first excuse. Find an activity that involves movement that you do enjoy. Dancing anyone?

I am happiness! I am health! I am wealth!

Aerial yoga at Jade Integrated Health in Brunswick, Maine.

ANDREW ESTEY

"Exercise is the single best thing you can do for yourself."

– ROBERT LUSTIG

STEP #3
Eat a Healthy Diet

The first step to eating healthfully is learning what really *is* healthy. There is a huge amount of myth-information about healthy eating in the U.S., some of it promulgated by the FDA, the government agency charged with the responsibility of keeping our food supply safe.

If your education about nutrition is over ten years old or nonexistent, it's time to brush up on what's new in nutrition. As a student nurse in the early sixties, I was taught that we didn't need to take vitamins, that we could get all the nutrients we needed from our diets.

I am happiness! I am health! I am wealth!

I no longer believe that to be true. One, agricultural practices have changed radically since then. We've heaped literally millions of tons of petroleum-based fertilizers, more tons of pesticides, and are now heavily applying tons of glyphosates to farm land. Every year we lose tons of topsoil and the nutrient value of the soil is diminished.

The meat in our supermarkets is primarily grown in farm factories, with animals living in cramped indoor spaces and eating corn and candy (Yes, candy! It's cheap and makes animals grow fat quickly — makes sense, if your goal is to get the meat to market as quickly and cheaply as possible. But, it will make you grow fat and sick quickly, too.) In addition, the animal likely was fed antibiotics, antibiotics that we then absorb. Those antibiotics are fostering the spread of antibiotic resistant infections.

Avoid faux foods! If your great grandmother wouldn't recognize a product in your supermarket as food, don't buy it. Faux foods will not make you healthy. In fact, the Standard American Diet, often abbreviated to SAD (my acronym: Sickness Activating Diet) is, to a great extent, responsible for the astronomical rise in the diseases that are plaguing us today: diabetes, obesity, Alzheimer's, spectrum disorders, arthritis, heart disease, cancer.

Recently, Tom Acklin, MD commented on "our Modern American Diet," which my brain immediately converted to MAD. That says it all. Our MAD is pure madness if you intend to be healthier next week or next year than you are today.

As kids, we said, "You are what you eat," intending the comment as an insult. Now, I see that as a basic guideline for soaring good health. Healthy foods will improve your health. Unhealthy, faux foods...

If you possibly can make it fit your budget, buy organic fruits and vegetables; buy organic, grass-fed meats, and free-range chickens who have not been penned up in egg factories. Americans now eat an ever-increasing number of meals outside the home, devastating to budgets and devastating to our health.

I am happiness! I am health! I am wealth!

A great resource for helping you decide which fruits and vegetables are most worthwhile to invest the extra money to buy organic is the annual list put out by EWG.org. There you will find the annual listings for the "dirty dozen." Strawberries typically top that list. They'll also give you the "clean fifteen." You'll find a fun page you can print and post on your refrigerator to help you make better produce choices. Your body will thank you.

ewg.org/release/out-now-ewg-s-2018-shopper-s-guide-pesticides-produce#.WwLYH4gvzIU

The average household spends an average of $3,008 per year on dining out, the Bureau of Labor Statistics reports.

cnbc.com/2017/09/27/how-much-americans-waste-on-dining-out.html

With regard to dining out, it's a healthcare nightmare out there. It is very difficult to get really healthy foods, although with increasing numbers of us demanding healthier foods when we dine out, it is getting better. One "danger" when dining out is portion size; over the past few decades servings have gotten bigger and bigger. Consequently, Americans and other western-style eaters have gotten bigger and bigger.

A good way to keep portions sizes reasonable is to split your entree, either by sharing with a friend or asking the server to box half of it to take home — before you start eating.

Another healthy strategy is to ask questions like: What is in this dish? What types of fats are in it? Can I have extra vegetables? Ask for EVOO — extra virgin olive oil — and vinegar for salad dressings. Avoid salad dressings with high fructose corn syrup, whether at home or eating out. The more questions you ask, the more control you have over what foods you are putting into your body.

What we term "health care" in the U.S. is really "disease care."

STRATEGIES

1. If you brown bag and eat primarily foods you prepare at home, you will save money and gain a whole lot more control over what you are putting into your body. If you are healthier, fewer of your dollars will be spent on health care.

2. There are some great books to help you learn what really is healthy food. (see *Rita Recommends* on page 94 for references and where to purchase) I love:

    The Immune System Recovery Plan by Susan Blum. MD, MPH

    The End of Alzheimer's: The First Program to Prevent and Reverse Cognitive Decline by Dale Bredesen, MD

    The Metabolic Makeover: It's All About Energy by Stephen Cherniske and Natalie Kather, MD

    Food: What the Heck to Eat by Mark Hyman, MD

    Genius Foods: Become Smarter, Happier, and More Productive While Protecting Your Brain for Life by Max Lugavere with Paul Grewal, MD

    Brain Maker: The Power of Gut Microbes to Heal and Protect Your Brain for Life by David Perlmutter, MD

    Medical Medium: Secrets Behind Chronic and Mystery Illness and How to Finally Heal by Anthony William

Medical Medium reveals the insights of a gentle man who, since childhood has been channeling health information from Spirit. It is not research-based, *but that does not mean it doesn't have real value!* My own health restoration was vastly advanced when I did his recommended 28-day detox plan in February, 2016. This book was the first step in my near-miraculous healing.

I use the term "near miraculous" deliberately. If I went to bed one night with only one leg and woke up the next morning with two fully functional legs, I'd call that miraculous. My own recovery was not quite that rapid; thus, my word choice, "near miraculous."

3. Stay current with new developments in the science of healthy eating. There is more and more information available at your local library or bookstore, on YouTube.com, or through webinars and local health care organizations. Here's a hot tip: Learn about vitamin K2. I'll bet you've never heard of it. K1 is the one you may well be familiar with; it is essential for blood clotting and is easily obtained from our foods.

"[K2] acts as calcium's shepherd, keeping it out of soft tissues, and in places where it should be, like bones and teeth," Max Lugavere explains in his book, *Genius Foods: Become Smarter, Happier, and More Productive While Protecting Your Brain for Life.* "Additionally, it 'activates' many proteins in the body and dietary intake of K2 has been linked with reduced cancer incidence, increased insulin sensitivity, better brain health and more."

A quick google gave me the following information: K2 is associated with a lower risk of heart disease, osteoporosis and dental disease, in addition to the benefits listed above. Sounds good to me!

healthline.com/nutrition/vitamin-k2#section7

4. DO NOT ASSUME that you know what is "healthy" when you shop for food! The books I just listed for you will give you a great start.

5. Start a book club based on these books. This will not only boost your knowledge; you'll form social bonds, a known boost to one's immune system, overall health and longevity.

6. Avoid processed foods like the plague. They are indeed causing an obesity/diabetes plague.

7. READ FOOD LABELS as if your life depended on it. It does. If the ingredients listed on a package contain words you can't pronounce or spell, put it back. Watch out for added sugar; it's everywhere in products you wouldn't imagine would contain sugar.

Would sugar by any other name taste as sweet?

According to the U.S. Dept. of Health and Human Services, added sugars show up on food and drink labels under the following names: Anhydrous dextrose, brown sugar, cane crystals, cane sugar, corn sweetener, corn syrup, corn syrup solids, crystal dextrose, evaporated cane juice, fructose sweetener, fruit juice concentrates, high-fructose corn syrup, honey, liquid fructose, malt syrup, maple syrup, molasses, pancake syrup, raw sugar, sugar, syrup and white sugar. Other types of sugar you might commonly see on ingredient lists are fructose, lactose and maltose. Fructose is sugar derived from fruit and vegetables; lactose is milk sugar; and maltose is sugar that comes from grain.

Less common names for sugar

The HHS list of sugar names is by no means exhaustive. According to the nonprofit Food Label Movement, there are almost 100 different names for sugar and sugar alcohols on ingredient lists. Some of the less apparent sugar names include carbitol, concentrated fruit juice, corn sweetener, diglycerides, disaccharides, evaporated cane juice, erythritol, Florida crystals, fructooligosaccharides, galactose, glucitol, glucoamine, hexitol, inversol, isomalt, maltodextrin, malted barley, malts, mannitol, nectars, pentose, raisin syrup, ribose rice syrup, rice malt, rice syrup solids, sorbitol, sorghum, sucanat, sucanet, xylitol and zylose.
healthyeating.sfgate.com/different-words-sugar-food-labels-8373.html

I dream of an app on my phone that could scan a package and give me a readout of what is really in the package.

"Sugar is the new white powder."

– ROBERT LUSTIG

STEP #4
Know What (and What NOT) to Eat

A STORY

When I was working as an RN in a weight loss clinic, our clients came in once per week for weigh-ins, one-on-one counseling and a group learning experience. Fairly often, I heard the comment, "I just want to be able to eat normally."

I am happiness! I am health! I am wealth!

Being the paragon of self-control that I am, I always resisted the urge to jump up and down on my desk, while shrieking, "NO!!!"

What I did say, calmly, "You DO NOT want to eat normally. Go to the mall and watch the people walking around there. The heavy ones, they eat normally. That is not what you want. In this country if you want to be a healthy weight, you have to eat *abnormally*.

That was in the late eighties. The folks in your local mall who eat "normally" today are much heavier than their predecessors.

Mom was right. Eat your vegetables! Lots of vegetables. A friend who spent some of his student days living among a tribe of hunter gatherers learned that they ate some 75 to 80 different plants every day! The typical American eats 11 plant foods per week! Most of them are potatoes and tomatoes. There is nothing wrong with either of those vegetables. But, we deplete their nutritive value by preparing them in the most common way, French fries and pizza sauce. We have an almost unlimited supply of fruits and vegetables from all over the planet and we choose to eat a tiny fraction of that vast array. To our detriment.

We are learning more and more about the nutrients and micronutrients contained in plants and how they can facilitate better health. Worse, we are learning more and more how our diets are literally killing us. Our forks and spoons have become weapons of mass destruction!

Max Lugavere's book (mentioned above and published six days before I started this book) is a great place to start.

I am happiness! I am health! I am wealth!

He lists the following foods as genius foods: extra-virgin olive oil, avocados, blueberries, eggs, grass-fed beef, dark leafy greens, broccoli, wild salmon, and almonds. Notice that six of those are plants. The grass-fed beef and eggs are not plants but are harvested from animals that ingest plants, so indirectly we are ingesting plants when we eat them.

Notice also that avocados, olive oil, salmon, and almonds are high in fat. If you are a senior, you were, without a doubt, indoctrinated with the attitude that fat is bad for us and that fat would make you fat.

Healthy fats do NOT make you fat. Sedentariness, high sugar intake, and manmade fats are the real culprits behind our soaring rates of obesity on this planet. Those obesity rates are fueling the lowering of life expectancy we are now seeing.

We currently hear a lot about the opioid epidemic, an affliction of truly devasting impact, both on the individuals who get caught in the opioid trap and on our society. The addictive processes in opioid addiction and sugar/unhealthy fat addictions are very similar. One significant difference is you can deliberately avoid all opioids; it is much harder to avoid the addiction-triggering foods in this country. They are everywhere!

You also were told not to eat eggs because they would cause heart disease. You were told not to eat shrimp because shrimp is high in cholesterol. You were told to eat lots of carbs; now we're seeing the long-term, very detrimental effects of high carb eating.

Your brain is primarily made up of phospholipids — lipids being fat. The truth is we were sold a bill of goods thirty or so years ago when we were taken on the low-fat ride.

Through the efforts of Ancel Keys in the sixties, Americans were taught that the fat in our diets, particularly the cholesterol in our diets, was causing heart disease, at the time the number one cause of death in the U.S. for both men and women.

Keys' study, *Seven Countries*, gained a lot of traction and had undue influence over health care for the next forty years. We went on a low-fat binge. And experienced an unprecedented rise in obesity, diabetes, and Alzheimer's!

I am happiness! I am health! I am wealth!

In Keys' day, authors were not required to publish the name of organizations from which they were taking money. Turns out that Keys was being paid by the Sugar Foundation. Frederick Stare of Harvard was also influential in promoting low fat diets; he, too, was receiving money from sugar producers/promoters.

What did Americans do during the low-fat decades? They ate a whole lot more sugar. Manufacturers and food producers added a whole lot more sugar because if they just removed the fat, the foods tasted bad, really bad.

Remember Snackwell's® cookies?

The pendulum always swings; now we know that fat, natural fats from fish and grass-fed, noncontaminated animals, is essential for our health. In fact, they are called "essential fatty acids," so named because they are essential for health, and our bodies cannot make them. We have to eat them.

Am I saying that, if you choose to be vegan or vegetarian, your diet isn't healthy? No, but I am encouraging you to be extra fastidious and knowledgeable about the food you put into your body.

I am happiness! I am health! I am wealth!

STRATEGIES

1. Do what you can to increase the number of organic foods in your diet. I learned this morning that Walmart is the largest supplier of organic foods. Who knew? Thrive.com will also help you meet your budget and eat healthier foods. Vitacost.com is another good source.

2. Inventory your pantry. Get determined and throw out all the processed products with unpronounceable names, the ones with sugar, (aim for less than 24 grams (6 tsp)/day if you are a woman, 36 grams (9 tsp)/day if you are a man), and the ones with high fructose corn syrup.

   Some of you are thinking, "I can't afford to throw away good food!" First let's be clear, foods with those ingredients are NOT "good food," they are FAUX FOOD. Here's your real choice: you can waste those foods or you can waist those foods. Because that is where they will end up, around your waist. Faux Foods make you fat and sick.

   It might cost you a bit of money to trash the Faux Foods, but it could well save your life.

3. DO NOT eat Faux Foods. And whatever you do, don't feed them to your kids and grandkids!

4. Explore the fun of new foods. Decide that each week when you shop for groceries, you will add one new real food to your cart. We have such a rich palette of available foods! On my list for this week is nutritional yeast. I've never bought it before. Then play with it by finding a recipe to add it to your plate.

5. Eat mushrooms! "All this taken together may explain why in an older adult population, mushroom consumption three or more times per week was associated with a 20% reduced risk of dementia." Sign me up! (Email from Max Lugavere, April 11, 2018)

6. It's very easy to think that taking steps to increase your health — buying organic, adding well-researched supplements to your life, hiring a personal trainer or getting that fitness club membership — is too expensive and decide, "I can't afford it." The real question is, "What price will I pay for NOT doing it?"

While we're on the topic of saving money...

7. If you improve your health, the money you currently spend on health care, doctor's visits, drugs costs, and the like will go down. You will be shifting costs from one category to another. You will open up new levels of health and happiness!

Personal statement: As I write this, I am cell-abrating the second anniversary of regular use of Univera products. Last week, I spontaneously told Anne, the nurse/nutritionist who introduced me to the products, "If you offered me a check for a million dollars, and I had to stop taking Univera products, I would tell you, "No deal!"

I am happiness! I am health! I am wealth!

"It's a pretty safe bet that any food product that contains more than five ingredients is highly processed."

– RANGAN CHATTERJEE

I scoop ice cream at work, but I don't eat it!

STEP #5
Add More Fun to Your Life

I am happiness! I am health! I am wealth!

A STORY

Two of my GRANDdaughters (I always cap the GRAND because they are so delightfully GRAND!) were visiting me for "Gramsie Camp." I woke up very early, much earlier than two soon-to-be teenaged girls. I snuggled into my chaise on the deck to drink my coffee and watch the sun rise.

When the girls woke up, I suggested that we all go swimming in our pajamas. We did — and it was an absolute blast!

I am happiness! I am health! I am wealth!

In January, 2016 as I was contemplating New Year's resolutions, it occurred to me that the reason most people fail at New Year's resolutions is we really want the end result (losing weight, getting more exercise and saving money being perennial favorites), but we don't want to do the work involved to get to that end result. What, actually go to the gym?!!! And sweat?!!!

I decided that from then on, I would set one intention, the same one every year for the rest of my life: to do something I have never done before in my life, just for the fun of it. Best New Year's intention I ever set.

Some of the things I have done: participated in a triathlon with a GRANDdaughter, went indoor sky diving with GRANDkids, got a pedicure with a GRANDdaughter, took the third GRANDdaughter to an aerial yoga class, hopped onto the tractor behind one of my brothers, went to a local high school production of *Les Mis*, played volleyball with both kids, their wives, and all four GRANDchildren.

In September, 2016, I participated in my first triathlon since 1992 (World Championship in Ontario, CA). I was racing as part of a team: doing the swim, with my GRANDdaughter Charlotte doing the bike segment, and her friend, Alyssa Colonnio, doing the run. We did it again in September, 2017, racing as the FabuLosees. We're signed up again and will be tri-ing with Charlotte's parents and younger sister, Caroline. Even more fun in store!

According to the rules I set up for myself, the activity I choose has to be only intended to be fun. I love aerial yoga; it's my newest passion. My first class didn't qualify as "just for fun" as I intended to get fitter during the class. And did!

I highly recommend setting the intention to do something NEW every month just for fun. Fun is good, life-enhancing. I get a happiness boost every time I do one of my fun experiences, I create memories that give me pleasure as I remember them. I bond emotionally with the folks who participate with me. I stimulate novel activities in my brain and body. Beneficial all around!

STRATEGIES

1. Write a list, the longer the better, of things that you love to do. Post it on your refrigerator as a reminder to add fun to your life.

2. Go to a laughter yoga class.

3. Watch old movies that make you laugh.

4. Adopt my intention of doing something you've never done before just for fun.

"Do things you love. Everyday."

– JAMES ALTUCHER

STEP #6
Keep Setting Goals: Things You Want to Be, Do, Have

A STORY

For many years I have declared myself a woman of InspirACTion, after realizing that the outrageous goals I'd set, like climbing Mt. Kilimanjaro and doing my first triathlon all happened because I was first inspired, then had taken action. When I put those pieces together, I declared myself to be a woman of InspirACTion — when inspired, take action. An inspiration without action is simply another breath.

None of the grand adventures of my life would have occurred if I had been unwilling to act on the inspiration. As a young student nurse in my obstetrical rotation, I watched women giving birth in the fashion of the day; drugged out of their minds, unconscious mostly, being lifted from the labor table to the delivery table, having their babies literally pulled from their bodies with forceps, the babies first held by doctors and nurses, not parents. The father's role was to be in the waiting room, smoking cigarettes, then passing out pink or blue cigars after he learned the sex of his newborn. As I write this, I feel a sense of how dreadful that way of giving birth was.

I am happiness! I am health! I am wealth!

During that same rotation, I took care of a woman who, the day prior to giving birth had gone horseback riding, and gave birth with no drugs, no anesthesia. What a gift she gave me! Although at the time, I wouldn't have termed it as being inspired, I was.

Eight years later pregnant with my first son, I took action and deliberately shopped for an obstetrician who would allow fathers in the delivery room and collaborate with us, enabling me to give birth without drugs, without anesthesia. That is what happened and it was truly one of the most extraordinary events of my life. To witness the birth of another human being is a profound and beautiful experience.

Without the inspiration of the woman I met as a student, I would never have been able to experience the raw beauty of being an active participant in the birth of my sons.

In my thirties, forties, and fifties, I had a goal habit. I was a BHAG lady, BHAGs being Big, Hairy, Audacious goals. I loved setting and getting goals. Bagged some great ones — did the Hawaii Ironman, stood on the summit of Mt. Kilimanjaro, hiked the Appalachian Trail, earned a doctorate, reared a couple of great kids, wrote lots of articles and a couple of books, became a polished public speaker. Then, BAM! It all got taken away.

I was ill when I returned from the Appalachian Trail. For years, I struggled to regain my health, doing what most of us would do, seeing doctors and taking medication. I was sometimes functional and sometimes not. I was able to hang on to my goal habit... most of the time.

 In January, 2010, I suddenly plunged into a major metabolic meltdown. Within days, I went from working, exercising, and putting the final touches on a book I was writing to feeling like I had been run over by a fleet of 18-wheelers.

I was unable to stand up. No, correction, I was unable even to sit up without feeling like I was going to faint. I had to lean on the kitchen sink while supporting my body with one hand in order to wash my cereal bowl. I certainly wasn't cooking. I was so brain fogged I didn't dare to drive. I was transformed into a couch slouch, slammed to the sidelines of my life.

I vividly remember one summer day when I needed to go to the library (wouldn't have survived without books!) and to the grocery store. I was so depleted, it took all my mental ability to get both errands done. While I was moving to get those two simple tasks accomplished, I carried on a continual debate in my mind about whether I had the stamina to get them both done. I vacillated throughout the time I was off the couch, feeling absolutely way-beyond-wasted, continually tempted to bag it and go home. Absolutely metabolically drained!

I did get those two errands done AND it took as much mental stamina and determination to do them as it did to run the last two miles of the Hawaii Ironman.

Even though I was off my goal game, I really did have an overarching goal: to get well. It took years, but here I am!

Here's my take on what makes a goal a good, worthy one. Do you just love the idea of doing it? Does it scrill you?

Scrill, is that a mistake? NO! Scrill is the word I created for the sweet spot of goal setting. Am I scared about what will be required to get this goal? Am I simultaneously thrilled about achieving it? If I am both scared and thrilled, I am scrilled and know I have good goals to put on my list.

I am happiness! I am health! I am wealth!

STRATEGIES

1. Start a Thirty-Year Goal Intention List (If you're in your fifties, make it at least a seventy-year list). That's a signal to the universe that you intend to play on planet earth for long after three score and ten.

2. Let your ideas flow as you create your list, as if you had no limits, not limited by time, energy, money. Make it a fun list!

3. Skip the bucket list. Make it a barrel list; buckets are way too small.

"If one goal that liberates and inspires you is good, why not set more? – RITA LOSEE

STEP #7
Get Your DHEA Up

I am happiness! I am health! I am wealth!

A STORY

What you don't know can hurt you. When I got slammed to the mat of my life in January, 2010, I had never heard of DHEA; couldn't have told you what it was if my life had depended on it. It turns out that my life — and your life — does depend on having adequate levels of DHEA-s ("s" stands for sulfate and is the more stable form of DHEA and the name for the blood test to ascertain DHEA levels).

One of the lucky things that happened to me when I was in the beginning of my metabolic meltdown years was seeing a DO (Doctor of Osteopathy, Patrick Mulcahy, DDS, DO) who measured my DHEA. When Dr. Mulcahy showed me my test results in the spring of 2010, I had virtually flat-lined in terms of adrenal glands. All of my adrenal hormones were virtually non-existent, including my DHEA.

The point of this particular story is that I, a long-time nurse and athlete, had NO IDEA about DHEA and how critical it is to health and well-being. The big mistake I made here: I didn't ask about DHEA and what impact it was having on my health. Why didn't I ask? There was an embarrassment factor operating; I, a long-time nurse, felt embarrassed that I was completely ignorant of DHEA. That embarrassment, and the totally depleted state in which I was living, was a block to my getting information that I desperately needed in order to restore my health.

You may not even know what DHEA is; most people don't. DHEA is a pro-hormone produced primarily in your adrenal glands, the two small endocrine glands that sit atop your kidneys. When we are in our early thirties, DHEA levels peak at about 350 for women and 450 for men.

Think about what you looked, felt, and acted like when you were thirty.

You had lots of energy. if you gained a bit of weight, it was relatively easy to get it off. If you got injured or sick, you recovered quite quickly. You went to sleep and stayed asleep without difficulty, your libido was high, you had zest and enthusiasm. You were vibrantly *alive*.

After peaking in our thirties, we produce about 2% less DHEA each year. If you are in your mid-seventies, you likely have only 10% the thirty-year-old-you had. DHEA is essential for cellular repair. If your cells are not repairing, cell by cell you and your body deteriorate. The average age of death is 78.4 years in the U.S. and *dropping*.

I am happiness! I am health! I am wealth!

There is a very significant correlation between DHEA levels and death rates. Can we state categorically that low DHEA causes death? No, but I'm staking my life, literally, on keeping my DHEA levels as close to what they were when I was thirty as I can.

From mid-2010 until mid-2016, my DHEA levels always registered <15. That means I had so little I wasn't even able to get on the scale used by that lab. Essentially, I had no DHEA.

And I had no life!

By mid-2016, my DHEA was up to 279. I had a life! I was exercising, working and having fun. I had energy!

The doc who was measuring my DHEA levels had ordered, and I was taking, supplementary DHEA for years. It wasn't until I started taking Prime, made by Univera, that my DHEA-s level went up. In April, 2016, my DHEA-s was still <15. After two months on Prime, my level was 279 and I had a life: more energy, more zest, more stamina.

Why haven't you ever heard about DHEA? Because, to quote Stephen Cherniske who literally wrote the book (*The DHEA Breakthrough*) on DHEA, "It's not a drug!" As a natural molecule, DHEA can't be patented.

In our pharmaceutically-driven medical world, doctors are not edu- cated about DHEA and its benefits, **even though there have been over 12,000 articles supporting the benefits of DHEA supplementation!** Those articles have been published in major medical journals, like the *Journal of the American Medical Association*.

I am happiness! I am health! I am wealth!

But, wait! There's more! We now have Prasterone. **Prasterone** is a man-made form of a hormone called dehydroepiandrosterone (DHEA), available since November, 2017. (Drugs.com)

Prasterone is used for the treatment of painful intercourse which is fairly frequent in postmenopausal women. I'm placing a bet here. The manmade form of DHEA is not as good as supplements that more closely mirror the nature-made type.

"Hey," you may be saying, 'If DHEA can help me look, feel, and act younger, I want some — today! I'm going to ask my doc to get tested." Perhaps not!

All too often, when patients ask for DHEA-s levels to be done, doctors refuse. This makes me very cranky! It's my body, I am directly or indirectly hiring that doctor to be a partner in my health. As far as I am concerned, no one, no matter how many degrees follow his name, has the right to tell me what to do with my own body.

`Let's go back to Prasterone. When it came out, I scurried off to my local pharmacy to ask what it cost. $268.39 for a 28-day supply! On June 1, 2018, the same pharmacy quoted approximately $225 per 28-day supply. Hmmm, if the month has more than 30 days, do I skip sex on those days?

So, here's my take on what the pharmaceutical companies' strategies are. They know about the research that supports supplementing with DHEA. But, who is their major market for pharmaceuticals? Seniors!

I am happiness! I am health! I am wealth!

"The percentage of Americans taking more than five prescription medications has nearly tripled in the past 20 years, according to the Centers for Disease Control and Prevention. And in our survey, *over a third of people 55 and older were taking that many drugs; 9 percent were taking more than 10.*" (*Consumer Reports*, Sept., 2107, italics mine)

This morning, reading the latest issue of *AARP Bulletin*, I came across this statistic: "Seniors take an average of 4½ prescription drugs each month..." (April, 2018, P 38) I was unable to find a statistic about how many over-the-counter drugs seniors take, but I'm betting the answer is, "A lot!"

In the U.S., we have a drug problem and it's not just the well-known opioid crisis.

My Prediction

They will manufacture "manmade" DHEA products focused on one of the multiple DHEA benefits and sell individual products for multiple profits. Prasterone costs **three times more than the DHEA supplement I take.**

I get systemic, whole body benefits from it, not just a happier vagina. Even if I overdose on Prasterone, it isn't going to help me have the energy to go out for a run!

STRATEGIES

1. Get a copy of *The DHEA Breakthrough: Look Younger, Love Longer, Feel Better* by Stephen Cherniske today. Then, talk with your healthcare provider.

2. While you are buying that, get *The Metabolic Makeover: It's All About Energy* by Stephen Cherniske and Natalie Kather, MD.

Come to think of it, I'm going to leave instructions to my sons to put a bottle of Prime (my favorite source of DHEA) into my casket — just in case!

3. Google the September, 2017 issue of *Consumer Reports* and learn how many Americans went to the Emergency Room in 2014 as a result of legally prescribed drugs.

4. Whenever you get prescribed a drug, do not take it until you have gone to drugs.com and thoroughly researched the side effects and adverse reactions. There is no way doctors and NPs can keep all that information in mind as they write your prescriptions. It's YOUR BODY and YOUR HEALTH!

5. When a doc suggests a drug, always ask, "Is there a life style intervention that will accomplish the same or better result?" If enough of us ask enough doctors, the health care industry will change for the better.

6. Instead of a PCP, primary care physician, seek out a PPP, a Patient Physician Partnership. Please note who got listed first in the statement.

7. Accept the fact that you may well have to educate your health care providers about DHEA; there is a high probability they won't know as much as you do after you've read *The DHEA Breakthrough.*

I am happiness! I am health! I am wealth!

"By age seventy-five, the decline in DHEA is approaching fatal. Without adequate DHEA the immune system, cardiovascular system, and brain start to malfunction. Tissue repair ceases, and death soon follows."

– STEPHEN CHERNISKE

STEP # 8
Say "No, Thanks"
to Living on a Fixed Income

A STORY

Many years ago, I was talking with a friend about my life pattern which had followed the cultural pattern of marrying and raising children. His observation was that by not working in a consistent career I had sacrificed the "best earning years of my life."

At that juncture, twenty-five years ago, I bought into that belief and accepted it as true. Based on earning statistics that still show women consistently earning and controlling less money than men do, that statement was objectively true. If you believe that to be true, it will be true for you.

Ask, "Is harboring that belief, continuing to hold it, beneficial for you?" Since the statistics and my own personal financial history strongly indicate it is very unbeneficial, I choose to no longer believe his statement. I now choose to believe that *I am now in the highest income years of my life.* After decades of believing I was "supposed" to live in a state of financial limitation, I am living in financial freedom!

Not infrequently, I hear seniors commenting, "I am living on a fixed income." My unspoken response is, "Why not fix it?"

I am happiness! I am health! I am wealth!

If you are happy with your current level of income, great, be happy with it. But, in the world where I live, the costs of the items I need and want are not fixed! Those keep going up. If you plan on living several more decades as I do, sooner or later, that fixed income is going to need fixing or it will become a limiting factor in your life.

Have you ever noticed that there is a correlation between retiring and starting to exhibit the signs and symptoms of aging? Have you ever heard of people, usually men, retiring and within a few months, getting sick and dying? I think that phenomenon is driven by decades of living in, and absorbing the belief that once you are beyond retirement, you are no longer useful, so you might as well get off the planet.

David Cameron Gikandi, the author of *A Happy Pocket Full of Money: Infinite Wealth and Abundance in the Here and Now*, concurs. He wrote, "Through retirement, they signal their brains and body that life is now wrapping up, coming to an end, and that society does not require their services any longer, so certain functions can now start to switch off." (P 81)

Jo Ann Jenkins, the CEO of AARP, observes, "Don't get me wrong: misperceptions and outdated stereotypes exist everywhere. But their impact is felt most strongly in Washington. It is a place steeped in the outdated view that getting older is about decline, that it presents challenges, and that older people are a burden society has to contend with, a drain on our communal resources."

I find it rather ironic that she cites Washington, D.C. as a place where the 4D (expectations of diminishment, deterioration, disease, and death) model of aging prevails. For as long as I can remember, there have always been older men occupying Congressional seats, well past the age of retirement.

It is my contention that the worst real estate for those "outdated stereotypes" to reside is in your head, heart, mind and soul. If you are completely steeped in, and fully aligned with, the belief that you (the only person whose beliefs you can control is you) are happy, healthy, productive and growing, participating fully in the growth of well-being on the planet, it really doesn't matter what others believe, whether they are in Washington, the White House, or your family.

I am happiness! I am health! I am wealth!

Jenkins points out that not only are these beliefs and stereotypes outdated, they are simply wrong. She cites Steve Gillon's (*Boomer Nation*) Longevity Economy (those 50 and older) as creating over $7.6 *trillion* annually in the economy.

Jenkins (P 28) comments, "For this generation of Americans fifty and older, the definition of the good life has shifted from owning a home, a nice car, and having a good job to place even more importance on good health, a financially secure future and satisfying relationships." Reading that line, my thought was, "Why not have all of the above in any amount you desire?"

There has been research done on the relationship between money and happiness. The findings are summarized by Lynne McTaggart in her newest book: *The Power of Eight* (p.184), "Unless you were poor, money just didn't do it for people." She continues, "People below that income level were miserable just because they were struggling to pay their bills, but once they'd achieved that level of income, making any more money didn't offer any greater joy."

The following quote sourced in the Government Accountability Office and cited in *Forbes*, is frightening: "...The truth is that as many as half of all households with Americans 55 and older have no retirement savings at all. Nothing. Zip. Nada. Not a dime."

forbes.com/sites/andrewbiggs/2017/01/18/are-half-of-americans-approaching-retirement-with-no-savings/#7167941140e5

In the last decade, the debt load for Americans aged 65 or older has skyrocketed by 83%, according to Federal Reserve.

I am happiness! I am health! I am wealth!

The Employee Benefit Research Institute notes 50% of seniors over the age of 75 still have outstanding debt.

kff.org/medicare/issue-brief/how-many-seniors-are-living-in-poverty-national-and-state-estimates-under-the-official-and-supplemental-poverty-measures-in-2016/

You will not be able to soar without adequate finances. I became acutely aware of how devastating it is to be ill and helplessly watch one's financial resources dwindle. I knew the financial stress was creating an unhealthy response in my body and because I was so ill, I couldn't turn it around for years. Fiscal distress and physical distress swirled though my life in an ever-escalating downward spiral.

On the morning after I thought I was completely finished writing this book, I found the term, "financial toxicity," in my latest *AARP The Magazine*. The article (June/July, 2018, P 50) focuses on how prohibitive financial costs of cancer treatments can interfere with healing. As someone who is still paying a debt left from a medical procedure done in April, 2016, I can attest to the fact that financial toxicity is not limited to cancer treatments. Financial toxicity is a frequent side effect of contemporary medicine.

In 2016, half of all people on Medicare had incomes of less than $26,200. I find that statistic appalling! I don't believe in the short term that public agencies will be highly active in helping seniors achieve a decent standard of living. It's pretty much up to us to fix our fixed incomes.

The idea of living on a fixed income conveys an underlying sense of lack and limitation. When I say, "fixed income," it implies that I am at the top of my income, that it is static and certainly not growing. If you are feeling lack and limitation, that will be your experience.

To start the process of fixing a fixed income, you might ask, "What do I love sharing with others? What do I love doing so much that I would do it for nothing? What do I know how to do that others will pay me for? What skills or knowledge do I have that others value and will pay for?"

A couple of years ago, I conceived the idea of "play for pay." My summer job at a local ropes course is so much fun, I am literally being paid to play there. I scoop ice cream (helps build muscle on my scooping arm!), help folks into and out of safety harnesses, and coach them in overcoming their fears. Making them feel welcome actually blends very nicely into my passion for living a life of adventure and sharing what I've learned. As I work, I am being a role modael for soaring.

I am happiness! I am health! I am wealth!

As I talk, I encourage folks to face, and overcome their fears. By virtue of my vintage, I inspire others to be physically active and fully engaged with life. Does that mean I don't work hard? Absolutely not! But simultaneously, it is playing for pay. One fun weekend last fall, I clocked 21 miles on my Fitbit over two days and woke up on Monday filled with energy and zest.

There are many relationship marketing companies that enable anyone, no matter one's age, to start a home-based business. Not only can one create a large and lucrative income stream with these companies, one also gets the tax advantages of being a business owner. Will it take work, time and effort to achieve financial freedom with these companies? Very likely, but the benefits of being a business owner are substantial. The side effects of being engaged in a business for which you have passion and commitment are fantastic!

Sixty-two percent of Americans want to start their own businesses.
nypost.com/2018/01/17/most-americans-dream-of-being-their-own-boss/

The beauty of relationship marketing businesses which are grounded in opening up business ownership opportunities is that there are huge numbers of folks searching for what you are offering.

I participate in two of these companies: Univera and Legal Shield; both offer unique, hugely beneficial products and have contributed greatly to my own life and well-being, both physically and fiscally.

Univera makes and markets the plant-based cellular regeneration products that enabled me to stop being a couch-slouch and get back to living! I knew within two months of using Univera's cellular regeneration products that I would be telling everyone I could about them. Given that, it only made sense to me to enroll as an associate and build fiscal health as I continued to build physical health.

Univera offers an online gift card. If you choose to use our products, the gift card will give you associate pricing for each item you order. For the first 90 days, you will get free shipping. And you also will receive a 90-day money back guarantee if you are dissatisfied in any way; save the bottles and your shipping statement. Customer service can provide labels for you to return empty containers.

In the interest of transparency, I will receive compensation if you choose to click on the link below and try our products. You will open a screen that asks for your redemption code. If you enter 20029884, your account will automatically be linked to me.
newunivera.com/giftcard

I am happiness! I am health! I am wealth!

Because I was a Legal Shield member, I was able to keep my home during the years when I was too disabled to work and was spending thousands of dollars a year in uncovered healthcare costs. I had disability insurance through my part-time nursing job; through that experience I learned that my insurer would do anything they could to help me — except pay my benefits!

I have had a Legal Shield membership since 2009 and fully intend to keep it for the rest of my life. In 2010, when my life crashed in my major metabolic meltdown, I, as an individual, was powerless. As an individual, I would have been denied the benefits I was legitimately entitled to and in all likelihood, would have become a long-term guest of a family member.

While I was devoting my energies toward getting well, Legal Shield was taking care of my rights to my insurance benefits. It took several months, but ultimately, I got a 5-figure settlement. My cost to maintain this service is $17.95 per month. I will keep it for the remainder of my life. The current pricing is $24.95. Legal Shield has never raised the price for an existing customer.

My Legal Shield address is: ritalosee.wearelegalshield.com.

If you are a senior, I fervently believe you have skills and abilities for which others will pay you. From where I sit, it seems that there will be ongoing challenges to social security and medicare programs, which most seniors rely upon. I hope those will remain intact, but isn't it always good to have options?

In the U.S., physical disability and fiscal disability are wrapped around each other like strands of DNA. The most frequent cause of bankruptcy is the high — and rising — costs of medical care. That statement alone indicates the desirability of continuing/creating growing income streams.

STRATEGIES

1. Ask yourself "What would I love?" I see more and more seniors working as I go about my world. This is a great question to ask yourself as you contemplate finding/creating new sources of revenue. (Thanks to Mary Morrissey who taught me that question.)

2. Write a list of skills you have or skills that you can develop that others would be willing to pay you for. Some that immediately come to mind are dogsitting, driving people, renting rooms in your home or with Airbnb, cleaning, writing letters, selling home cooked foods (check health regulations here), tutoring, writing/selling a book.

3. Consider a relationship marketing business for a product you love.

"Money is a byproduct of being a good, competent, creative, healthy person."

– JAMES ALTUCHER

Swimming with dolphins.

STEP # 9
What You Think About and Talk About Comes About

I am happiness! I am health! I am wealth!

A STORY

Ever hear someone say, "That sounds too good to be true?" Of course, you have. But, did you ever hear someone say, "That sounds *too bad* to be true?" I'll bet not. That illustrates our human "negativity bias."

Recently, I mentioned a "good" outcome I was observing. The woman I was speaking with replied, "Now you've jinxed yourself." She went on to say that I would now soon experience the negative outcome I was celebrating not having.

As I mused upon that interaction, I sensed how deeply we, as a culture, believe in undesired outcomes more strongly that positive outcomes. If the thoughts we have today are integrally woven into the experiences we will have tomorrow, or at some future date, it is to our benefit to shift our thoughts and underlying beliefs.

Einstein is quoted (or sometimes perhaps misquoted) as saying, "The most important question facing humanity is, "Is the universe a friendly place?" The underlying premise of the belief about "jinxing" yourself by mentioning an outcome you favor is a clear indication of seeing the universe as an unfriendly place.

How many thoughts did you have yesterday? About 50,000 give or take a few thousand. According to any number of sources I've accessed over a couple of decades, everyone has that many thoughts every day!

Please don't ask me how they did the research! But, based on what goes on in my head, I know we generate huge numbers of thoughts every day.

What percent of those thoughts are negative? About 79%! Yikes! That's a lot of Eeyore thinking! There is a very good reason why our brains have "negativity bias." Eons of time ago, when our species was scraping for survival and the major challenges were about surviving for the day — getting a meal rather than becoming a meal — being wired to see the negative, the dangers around us, kept us alive.

That negativity bias can be a really good thing! I, for one, am very grateful that my ancestors survived to propagate.

Like everything else in life, there seems to be a sweet spot where there is a balance. In the case of your thoughts, you want the balance to be on the positive side because what you think about and talk about comes about. Most of the world's spiritual traditions and now, quantum science, attest to the truth of that statement.

I am happiness! I am health! I am wealth!

What percent of our thoughts are repetitive? NINETY-FIVE PERCENT! If thoughts are creative, then what we think about and talk about today is influencing what we experience in the future. We need to pay attention to our thoughts. Even more, we need to be in charge of our thoughts!

What thoughts create happiness when you think them? Those are the ones to think, frequently and often! Health? Wealth? Think about and celebrate/appreciate every bit of health, wealth and happiness you now have. That healthy, happy, wealthy energy will create more health, wealth, happiness, actively playing a part in bringing more of the same — no matter how many trips you've made around the sun in this lifetime.

As I've aged, I have noticed the tendency of my peers to answer the stock question, "How are you?" with a list of bodily complaints, along the line of, "My back hurts," "I just got out of the hospital," "I'm going to have surgery for..." The sensations of sickness can be so all-consuming they take over your life and body. I didn't know how to keep focused on health and well-being when the most dominant awareness was such devastating illness. Virtually no one does.

My training as an endurance athlete was helpful; it gave me insight into the process. As an athlete, there were many times when I deliberately chose to ignore the messages I was getting from my body to quit, or slow down, or back off. In the service of my goal of finishing a race, I chose to focus in finishing, not the protests of my body.

Ever so slowly, I learned to focus on my goal of getting well, changing what I could, and affirming, in spite of the evidence, that my body was fully capable of healing.

Getting out of the habit of talking about my illnesses was a really tough challenge. It's very hard to think about much else except those gaw-dawful feelings emanating from sick cells, including brain cells, and organs. I didn't know how when I first started.

It was so natural and normal to complain when others lovingly asked about my well-being. Over time, and with the practice of listening to myself, I began to shift my response to the stock question, "How are you?" I learned to say, "Terrific!" Or "Great!"

And, when I started focusing on what was going well in my body, the energy began to shift — as did my health. Faith/belief precedes evidence. Today's experiences/evidence are the result of the thoughts, ideas, beliefs that I've thought in the past. If I want to change my experiences, the first step is to change my thoughts and beliefs and celebrate having them now. That is where your imagination comes in.

There is a growing body of research that establishes that our brains have no ability to detect a difference between something "real" and something vividly imagined.

I remember the beginning of my Appalachian Trail through-hike, hiking through Georgia with over 2000 miles to go to reach my goal of standing on the summit of Mt. Katahdin in Maine. As I walked along, I'd imagine what it would be like to reach the summit of Katahdin. It was such a powerful imagining it brought tears to my eyes. Envisioning standing on the summit of Mt. Katahdin immediately brought an upsurge in my energy and enthusiasm. The actual experience was even better than the imagined ones.

I am happiness! I am health! I am wealth!

While earning my doctorate and feeling overwhelmed by all that needed to be done, I'd often imagine what it would be like to slip into that gorgeous scarlet robe and be at graduation. If you intend to get a doctorate, make sure the gown of your university is a color you love!

When anyone asks me today how I am, my answers vary. "Terrific!" "Soaring!" "Fantastic!" At first, there was a very large space between terrific and what the sensations in my body actually were. Currently, when I say "I am feeling terrific, that is my reality. I also often say, "I am getting better every day!"

"In the beginning was the Word…" My words of being "terrific" and the like were the beginning of the soaring experiences I am now living. What you think about and talk about comes about. I am so grateful!

"Another bonus of gratitude is faith. By being grateful now for the things you intend to experience in the future, you become ever more certain that you will experience them, and this in turn brings them to you. It allows you to be excited about the future." (Gikandi, P 179)

I am health. I am wealth. I am happiness.

Ironman finish (age 46).

Appalachian trail finish (age 58).

STRATEGIES

1. Love your body, no matter what is "wrong" with it. Having grown up with the belief that my body was "wrong" in so many ways: not thin enough, not beautiful enough, thighs too fat... I now treat my body as something I truly love and treasure. After all, this body has taken me on so many fantastic adventures and continues to do so! I am so grateful!

2. Meditate. Short (and free) meditations I love can be found at your-resonant self.com. Sarah Peyton's one cell meditation gifts you a way to gently increase your love for your body.

3. Be kind to yourself. Remember, every cell in your body hears what you say and think about it. Obviously, our cells don't have ears, but they are all sensitive to, and aware of, the vibrations of our thoughts.

   Words and thoughts themselves carry energy. "I love you!" carries a very different energy/vibration than "I HATE You!" If you, as so many of us do, feel negatively about your body, your body's cells are responding negatively as well.

   Please don't ever talk about having a "senior moment;" that literally is programming your own brain to get a result you definitely do not want.

4. Be grateful. A challenge for you: How many times in a day can you sincerely think, "I am grateful for _____"? The more you can retrain your brain to think and feel gratitude, the more events will occur that will cause you to be even more grateful.

Sow a thought, and you reap an act;
Sow an act, and you reap a habit;
Sow a habit, and you reap a character;
Sow a character, and you reap a destiny.

Charles Reade

STEP #10
Keep Learning
What if You Learned Something New Every Day?

STORY

I stood on the summit of Springer Mountain, Georgia, contemplating the goal I had set, to hike all the way to the summit of Mt. Katahdin, Maine. I was a very inexperienced hiker/backpacker. Yes, I'd done a lot of camping, I'd done technical rock-climbing, I had done some day hikes. I had never backpacked day after day for well over two thousand miles.

There was so much I didn't know! Starting with I didn't know if I was going to like the experience.

I am happiness! I am health! I am wealth!

The Appalachian Trail is a great learning laboratory. There are people there with lots of experience who love to talk about the best way to... There are others, like me, who are complete neophytes. There is a lot to learn. Geography, the history of the areas we were hiking in, where the best bunks were in the trail towns, which restaurants featured all-you-can-eat buffets, where the best views were.

One of the most freeing aspects of the Trail is the tradition of trail names. Folks don't even typically go by their given names, but are known as "Pudding", "Coloradoo", "Camo" and "Never Again". Leaving one's name is a way of leaving one's history. No one really cares what your job title is, how much money you make, or what your education level is — all hallmarks by which we put one another into slots.

On the Trail, those aspects are irrelevant, freeing hikers up to be open to new experiences and learning. Freeing us up to be kids.

One of the most delightful experiences I have had is witnessing the passionate drive for learning that my kids and GRANDkids exhibited as little ones. May they NEVER LOSE that drive! How absolutely delightful that as they get older, I can learn from them!

One of the thought habits we seem to develop as we get older is getting stuck in thought ruts. Surely, you had a grandparent who told you the same stories over and over. There are likely physiological, lifestyle reasons for that all-to-common happenstance. Another possibility is that the person is not getting much stimulation from new activities, new challenges, new experiences. There is an expression about a grave being only a deep rut, with the ends closed in. Whether of thoughts or behaviors, ruts diminish our capacity for growth. Why put yourself in any kind of rut when you've got a living, breathing body?

What if your intention was to learn something new every day? It doesn't have to be a big effort. It doesn't have to require a lot of time. It doesn't require a lot of effort.

"Use it or lose it," applies to brain cells just as it does to muscle cells.

I am learning how to be a super successful associate with Univera. That endeavor keeps me learning; I am learning a lot about how to live a very healthy life no matter how old one is! For many decades as a long-time nurse and endurance athlete, I have been fascinated by the human body and how it functions. Right now, we know more about health and well-being than ever before in all the time humans have ever lived. The pace of our new learning is catapulting. How exciting!

And, very practical, too! Knowing how to facilitate healthier cells has made an exponential increase in my health and well-being.

This ongoing learning gives me a great opportunity to do something I love! Lead and inspire!

I am happiness! I am health! I am wealth!

Earlier this morning, I spent time reading and taking notes from a new (to me) book, *Sales Scripting Mastery: The 7-Step System for Consistently Delivering Successful Sales Presentations* by Eric Lofholm.

Learning how to be more effective at sales will provide great benefits to me as I inspire others to live healthier, wealthier lives.

Now, your intention doesn't have to be in service of a vision such as the one I have. Perhaps, your intention for learning something every day is only to keep your own brain functioning at a high level. Great! That's the only reason you need!

STRATEGIES

1. Repetition is a basic principle of learning. Keep repeating what you learn until you own it. A great way is to share what you learn with others. Writing and/or speaking your new knowledge requires additional brain cells, thus wiring more nerves into the circuits in your brain, consolidating the learning.

2. Learn from those around you. People love to share what they know and everyone knows something interesting. Most of us over fifty have a wealth of interesting thoughts, stories, experiences, and insights to share. Ask questions and you'll find folks love to share their knowledge.

3. Get enough sleep! During sleep is when your brain transfers new, temporary learning into long-term storage.

4. Please don't talk about your insomnia. We've been socialized to expect to have insomnia when we are seniors — as have the doctors we see. Don't buy into the idea that it's normal and okay to be a sleep-deprived senior. It's pretty normal for people of all ages to be sleep-deprived but it is not optimal, not by a long shot.

5. DO NOT start taking prescription drugs for insomnia without trying EVERYTHING else first. They cause some rather nasty side effects. To check the side effects of any drug; drugs.com is a great place to start your research.

STEP #11
Get a Good Night's Sleep

STORY

I was a champion sleeper! My entry into the Sleeping Hall of Fame was gained while on safari in Africa. Our group was camped in an area so wild the guides would only permit me to run in a very confined area, within their sight.

There were about fourteen of us, all sleeping in tents. As evening came on, we gathered around a big campfire for warmth and safety. We watched the spooky gleam of hyenas' eyes as we sat by the leaping and crackling fire as night fell. We all turned in early. The next morning my husband asked, "Did you hear the trucks running at the tents last night?" I had not. He continued to talk about how there were three trucks who had driven directly at out tents with drunken drivers yelling epithets at us.

He insisted it had happened. I didn't believe him and decided he was playing a practical joke on me — until the other campers emerged from their tents, talking about how frightening the incident was! I slept through the whole thing!

As a student nurse, I was taught that it was normal for seniors to get less sleep. That does seem to be true, but what they neglected to say that not getting enough sleep is very detrimental to one's health. Now, we know better.

I am happiness! I am health! I am wealth!

The real problem here is that if medical professionals and the public expect seniors to have sleep disorders, that becomes a self-fulfilling prophecy and when it happens, it is not addressed as a problem that needs remedial actions.

We know that our bodies need to replace some 300 billion cells every single day. When does the repair/replacement take place? At night, when we are sleeping! Diminished sleep. Diminished repair. *No sleep. No repair.*

We know if we don't repair our cars, eventually they break down and need to be replaced. Somehow, we've adopted that attitude toward our cells. Replacing our body parts is big business! But they don't — and never will — work as well as the ones we were born with!

Sleeping soundly and deeply is absolutely essential for living full-out. Folks who get inadequate sleep are more likely to be obese, to develop diabetes, and to overeat. They are less likely to exercise because they don't have enough energy and exercise all too often causes pain; both discomfort/pain while they are exercising, and stiffness and soreness afterwards.

I am happiness! I am health! I am wealth!

Getting your seven to eight hours of good sleep every night is essential to your well-being.

Very recently, I read in Max Lugavere's book, *Genius Foods*, that we have a glymphatic system in our brains. He states, "this system forcefully pushes cerebrospinal fluid through the brain while we sleep, providing a free power-wash for our brains every single night." (P 249) Guess it's a great idea to keep a clean brain as well as a clean house.

I also recently read that our gastrointestinal system undergoes a powerful wave of energy from stem to stern that clears our GI system every night. Again, one needs to be asleep for this cleaning action to occur.

High levels of stress and low levels of sleep go hand in hand. Take time to unwind before bedtime, which ideally should be at the same time every night. Most authorities advise using your bedroom for sleep or sex; we develop a Pavlovian response that will assist us in getting to sleep.

I add two other activities to the "okay in the bedroom" list; writing a list of three to five experiences from the day for which you feel grateful.

That simple exercise will reduce your stress and shift you out of your brain's inherent negativity bias.

The second activity that is high on my list is cuddling into my bed and reading. I find it a most delightful way to send myself off to the land of nod. If you have a partner or pet in your bed, or in your life, cuddling before bed is a great way to settle into a good night's sleep. Cuddling/ eye contact with those we love releases oxytocin, the bonding hormone Mother Nature uses to bind mothers and babies. Vitamin O, as it is sometimes called, sends cascades of positive sensations and reactions through our bodies. Get as much as you can!

Darken your bedroom as much as you possibly can. Melatonin, levels of which rise in the evening, is the hormone that we need in order to sleep. Light shuts down the production of melatonin. Our ancient ancestors and those not-so-ancient went to bed at dusk and rose with the sun. Only with the advent of electric lights did that average person have the light necessary to enable night time activities.

We're not going to revert to that dusk/dawn pattern, but we do need to do all we can to help our pineal glands do their jobs, get melatonin in action. If there is too much ambient light in your neighborhood to really darken your bedroom, get blackout shades or eye masks.

Turn off your electronics an hour before bedtime. If you use your computer or other electronic devices, get blue blocker glasses to modify the light that seems most incompatible with sleep.

I am happiness! I am health! I am wealth!

What deleterious impact does sleep deprivation (less than seven to eight hours) have on your body? M. Walker, in his book, *Why We Sleep: Unlocking the Power of Sleep and Dreams,* has much to say on that topic.

1. Down-regulates your immune system, "more than doubling your risk of cancer." (P 3)

2. Increases risk of Alzheimer's disease.

3. Increases blood sugar levels. Short intervals of sleep shift the metabolism of healthy individuals into prediabetes.

4. Increases the likelihood of heart attack, stroke, and congestive heart failure.

5. Reduces the ability to control eating while at the same time increasing drive for high sugar, inflammatory foods.

6. Increase the likelihood of obesity while simultaneously reducing the likelihood of exercising.

7. Decreases the effectiveness of your annual flu shot.

8. Blocks the glymphatic systems, nightly cleansing of your brain.

9. Impedes transfer of short-term memory into long-term memory.

10. Increases emotional reactivity and impairs rational decision-making.

11. "...contributes to all major psychiatric conditions, including depression, anxiety and suicidality." (P 3)

12. Greatly increases the likelihood of traffic accidents and fatalities.

13. Increases mortality and morbidity in the elderly, "the lower an older individual's sleep efficiency, the higher the mortality risk." (P 97)

14. Impairs replication of DNA and shortens telomeres (shorter telomeres are correlated with shorter life span.

15. Reduces testosterone and libido.

Question: If I had a pill that would reduce all those risks, what would you pay me?

Answer: *Anything I asked.*

STRATEGIES

1. If a health care practitioner wants to you start taking prescription drugs for insomnia, please proceed VERY carefully. Start by going to drugs.com and really read the side effects possible. Do you want to take those risks?

2. Then, turn on your television and watch the evening news. Skip the news, guaranteed to be bad — "if it bleeds it leads." But, do watch the commercials. You will encounter a glut of drug ads and hear the voiceover of possible adverse events. Really listen to those threats to

both your health and wealth. Again, ask: do I really want to take those risks? Getting into my car and driving around without any conscious memory of doing so?

I recently read those who take sleeping pills only sleep for an additional 11 minutes per night. Not worth either the risk to your health or your wallet in my opinion.

3. Don't argue with family members in the evening; stress will exacerbate any difficulty in falling asleep.

4. If you do find yourself ruminating on your worries, set aside a daily appointment with yourself to worry, say from 8:00–8:30 am. If you start worrying at any other time, write down the worry, and tell yourself, "I'll worry about that in the morning. Right now, I am going to blissfully drop off to sleep." Keep your appointment with yourself.

5. Use your worry appointment whenever you find yourself worrying. Do put if off until tomorrow.

6. Don't use alcohol as a sedative. One of the hidden illnesses of seniors is alcoholism; it's likely that many start or increase their alcohol consumption as a sleep aid. It will help you fall asleep, but it will also cause middle of the night awakening, as well as liver disease.

As a senior, your liver is not as adept at clearing out metabolic by-products and toxins as it was when you were younger. Alcohol is not processed/cleared as efficiently. Your liver is already challenged in today's *Faux Food*/toxin/stress-laden environment. You need healthy liver cells.

We are now experiencing an explosion in the incidence of non-alcoholic fatty liver disease which is caused by the bad old American diet. Too much sugar, too much high fructose corn syrup, too many unhealthy fats, and too many highly processed Faux Foods are wreaking havoc on our bodies.

7. Try M & M: meditation and masturbation. If you have a partner, even better! Sex works! Both work marvelously well for helping one get to sleep. Both are very relaxing, both separate our minds from the anxiety that is so often causing our insomnia in the first place.

"If sleep does not serve an absolutely vital function, then it is the biggest mistake the evolutionary process ever made."

– ALLEN RECHTSCHAFFEN

STEP #12
Experience Jolts of Joy Every Day

A STORY

As I write this, I am sitting on my bed in my RV, listening to big splats of rain hit the roof. The air is soft and moist as it drifts across my skin from the open window inches from my head. At times, the wind picks up and tosses the tree branches around the camper, creating a staccato rhythm of much more rain dashing against the roof. I am so cozy and warm, so enjoying what I am doing and am filled with joy. Simple delights creating great joy and gratitude. My entire life is enriched by them.

I am happiness! I am health! I am wealth!

Children know how to execute this step easily and effortlessly!

"An apple a day..." Without a doubt, the words that follow "day," rolled automatically off your tongue.

Another way to keep the doctor away is to be joyful! With antidepressants being a huge source of income for pharmaceutical companies, ("clinical depression affects about 16 million people in the U.S. and is estimated to cost the U.S. about $210 billion a year in productivity loss and health care needs." time.com/4900248/antidepressants-depression-more-common/) Americans by the droves are relying on synthetic substances for feeling good! NOT. Go to drugs.com and check out the side effects on any drug that is prescribed! Ask yourself if any substance that has those side effects will increase your joy level.

Make a list of the things that bring you joy. Make it an extensive one. Make it a point to seek out, notice and appreciate those moments of joy. Yesterday, my jolts of joy experiences came from the vibrant red of the strawberries I bought, the delicious smell of the Easter lily on my coffee table, stepping outside my door and hearing birds sing, the warmth of the sun on my back, the sight of deep purple crocuses along the foundation of my neighbor's home, the warm smile of the woman who checked out the groceries for me, a grin and hug from a disabled child.

The list can be endless! The trick is to notice and appreciate those little jolts of joy!

As I write this, I am becoming aware that another awful part of being so ill for so many years was the low level of jolts of joy in my life. But, even then, I found them in things I could watch from the sidelines of life, the delight of a sunrise, the sight and smell of flowers, receiving badly needed money.

Nike's recommendation applies here: JUST DO IT!

I am happiness! I am health! I am wealth!

STRATEGIES

1. Take pictures of your sources of jolts of joy. You can revisit them as often as you wish.

2. Post them on your Facebook page and share the joy.

3. Visit friends' Facebook pages and participate in their joy. Sometimes the jokes I find in mine are pretty funny, too.

4. Go to YouTube and watch videos that inspire you, intrigue you or uplift you in some way! There is some marvelous stuff out there.

5. Start a jolts of joy conversation/club with friends. Ask everyone to start each conversation with sharing jolts of joy.

"You are not happy because of certain conditions; certain conditions come into being because you are happy."

– DAVID GIKANDI

Learning to hoverboard.

STEP #13
Have Soup for Breakfast

STORY

As I mused about what story to start this step with, I started to remember really memorable meals. Some of them were traditional, like Christmas dinners and our family Fourth of July Lobster and Clam feed. The ones that really stood out were unusual meals, such as playing pancake "frisbee" with the kids when they were young.

Another very memorable meal was served on a chilly beach in Florida while we were mid-winter camping with the boys. We bought a half gallon of ice cream and sat on a bench overlooking the beach. Each of us had a spoon; we shared the whole carton for lunch.

I haven't eaten ice cream in the last couple of years and am far healthier because of that change. But, could I see myself reprising that fun meal with GRANDkids? Oh, yes!

I am happiness! I am health! I am wealth!

Does soup for breakfast sound like a nutty idea to you? Great, it's always good to shake up your routine (see Step #3).

In addition, there are some sound health reasons for having soup, or other unconventional foods, for breakfast.

1. This is the quickest way to boost the nutritional value of your breakfast. The cereal/bagel/muffin/cup of coffee as I dash out the door style of many westerners is a health disaster.

   We need a VARIETY of foods in order to maximize our health. A hot bowl of vegetable soup (or two) instantly gives you a whole bunch of vegetables early in the day!

2. The best soup is the soup you make yourself. When you have time (if you're thinking, "I'm too busy, I don't have time," ask yourself at precisely which time it would be convenient to have a serious illness). If you MUST buy soup, read the labels very, very carefully. It's a jungle out there!

3. One of my favorite soups is "refrigerator soup." As a single woman who cooks for one, I find that all too often, I have leftover fresh vegetables quietly converting themselves to compost in my refrigerator. Once a week to stop the waste, I go through the refrigerator, pulling out whatever vegetables I find and toss them into a soup pot, along with onion and garlic, plus whatever protein sources I might have on hand, sometimes meat, more often beans and lentils. I add water to cover and, if I have any vegetable or chicken stock on hand, pour that in. After bringing it to a boil, I let it simmer while I go about my life.

I get a variety of vegetables all in one bowl, avoid wasting perfectly good vegetables, and have several meals worth of soup waiting for me when I'm hungry. Fast food at its finest.

"No one ever brings a large tossed salad to the table and says to the people gathered there, 'I just made you the greatest salad because I love you so much!'"

– RITA LOSEE

STEP # 14
Get Your Will Done!

STORY

My maternal grandfather left the property where I now spend summers to his children, "to share and share alike." The intention was that they each enjoy this land that had been in our family for generations.

The problem was that his six children were geographically scattered across the U.S. from Maine to Alaska. Some were married with spouses who had less of a connection to this acreage. What an emotionally trying and completely disrupting family drama ensued! Long latent sibling rivalries appeared. Stuff from childhood, the whole process got quite messy and emotionally distressing for all concerned.

I am happiness! I am health! I am wealth!

Fortunately, we did arrive at what for many of us was a good resolution. Family members still hold this beautiful land on the coast of Maine. My understanding decades later is how very important it is to have a will and to be ever so careful in how it is structured.

According to Connie Ayotte, a Legal Shield associate, 85 percent of Americans don't have a will! That is astonishing since 100% of us are going to die. Dying will-less is a recipe for fiscal disaster waiting to trap your loved ones in an expensive legal mess. You want those who love you and survive you to miss you, not be furious because you left them in an emotional/legal can of worms.

What's the number one reason folks don't want to do a will? It's because they don't like the idea of dying. So, we just go along pretending it's not going to happen to us. WRONG!

I have no anticipation of dying today! But, I will be driving...

Since we never know when we'll die, it's a good idea to get your will done. Think of it as a love letter.

The second reason why folks don't get a will done is because they "don't have the money." Are lawyers expensive? Typically, yes, if you think a couple hundred dollars an hour is expensive. But, without a will, it's all too likely your loved ones will be hiring one, or many, because you didn't. Worse, they may end up fighting with each other, surely not a legacy you wish to create.

Here's the best way (and cheapest!) to get your will done. Go to ritalosee. wearelegalshield.com. It will cost you $24.95/month. Both you and your spouse/partner will get an individualized will done; one you can update free of charge every year.

I am happiness! I am health! I am wealth!

There are several other benefits of Legal Shield membership; If you get audited by the IRS, they've got you covered. (I'm working on my taxes right now; perhaps that's why I tagged this one!)

BTW, there is no contract with Legal Shield, so you won't be stuck if you want to drop it.

When I was disabled, my disability company declined for quite some time to pay my legitimate benefits. I cynically say, "I discovered my disability company would do anything they could to help me get well, except pay my benefits." Because I had a Legal Shield membership, I got a five-figure settlement and stayed out of bankruptcy court. I'll keep that membership for the rest of my life!

STRATEGY

In the immortal words of Nike: JUST DO IT.

"In your life, though you may not know it, you create your experiences first in your self, spirit, being, then in your mind, then by your words, and finally by your actions."

– DAVID GIKANDI

STEP #15
Forgive Yourself and Others

A STORY

My ex-husband and I were at the DMV, not on any day a place where I'm really hot to go. We were there to complete the transition of my car into my name with a new license plate. By this time, Grid and I had worked through a lot of the divisive anger that led to our divorce. We were so easy with each other that the woman who was behind the counter commented on how remarkable our behavior was and complimented us.

We went outside with my new plates and Grid took the time to attach them to my car. A generous, forgiving act on his part.

I am happiness! I am health! I am wealth!

If you are old enough to be reading this book, you've done some not-so-nice things to yourself or to others. You've made mistakes and been less than loving or pleasant at times. Maybe even downright hostile and destructive to others.

See your mistakes as a movie director would, as mis-takes. If you don't like how an episode in your life played out, decide to re-shoot that episode, changing it until you love the results.

One of the quickest ways to re-shoot any episode is to start with forgiveness. First, forgive yourself for doing whatever it was that caused the situation(s) you are concerned about.

You could start a "People I Am Choosing to Forgive" list. Devote a few minutes each day to focusing on one person/action and quietly send them loving kindness energy. In your mind and heart, ask for forgiveness. In this world of endless energy, it doesn't matter whether the others are dead or alive, finding peace and forgiveness is the intention. Intentions matter.

ASK is an acronym. Accessing Someone's Kindness. The "S" can also stand for "Spirit's." Your choice.

No one gets to be perfect in their earthly experience. That means we all have done things to others that warrant forgiving. A good exercise is to find a trusted confidant and share with them the items on your list. Doing that feels hard but really is an unburdening. You will feel lighter in the same way you do after carrying something heavy and putting it down.

I am happiness! I am health! I am wealth!

If you can, find a means of making restitution. Many years ago, one of the high schoolers who worked at my family's Dairy Queen and who was left in charge during the dinner hour called us long after she had moved into adulthood. It seems she had given cones to classmates while in charge. She came back and worked for nothing to make up the financial deficit she had created for us. I know that reaching out was hard for her. But, her action created good will and forgiveness all around.

The most important result was that her action gave her the ability to forgive herself.

An important attitude to adopt when viewing mistakes — ours or someone else's — is that what we do makes perfect sense from our perspectives, histories, experiences, fears, and woundedness. People don't act irrationally even when their actions are irrational!

As I retrospect my parenting, I can see actions and attitudes that I can directly trace to experiences that I had while I was being parented. Things that I can see were not in the best interests of the kids I was parenting. Nor mine. I modeled myself after my own parents, as we all do, either consciously or unconsciously. The operative word here is *unconsciously.*

As a female, my parenting style was, in some important ways, modeled on how I had been mothered. I had a good mother who did many things very well. But, not everything. I unconsciously replicated those aspects of her parenting, too. As we all do!

I wasn't aware at the time of that modeling. Thus, I certainly can't reasonably hold myself as guilty of being less than I was. I can acknowledge that if I had known then what I now know, my behaviors would have been different.

I can let my kids know that I wish I had been better able to be a better parent, that I now see changes that if I could roll back the clock, I would make. Here's what I understand — and hope: that when my sons get to be my age, they, too, will understand more than they do now. I consider it will be a blessing, if retrospectively, they can understand more about growth and increasing effectiveness than they do now. I hope they look back and think, "I know stuff now I didn't know then. I'd be a better _____ (fill in the blank) now." That's just evolution in action.

I am happiness! I am health! I am wealth!

STRATEGIES

1. If you haven't been learning anything in the past few decades, you haven't really been living. You've just been existing and occupying space on the planet. What if you deliberately started to learn something new today?

2. Ask yourself: "What would I LOVE to learn?"

3. Refuse to be embarrassed by what you don't know. There is no such thing as a stupid question; there are simply things you don't know.

4. When you meet anyone, play a game to see if they know something you don't. Then ask them to explain it to you. People generally LOVE to share their passions with others. You both win.

5. Practice Ho'opono'pono. If you don't know what that is, Google it.

"When you are a source of forgiving, you become a target for getting."

– RITA LOSEE

STEP #16
Grow Things

A STORY

When my older son was small, I was in my "earth mother" stage, growing a big organic garden which got larger every year. My fantasy when he was a toddler was that we would spend happy hours working in the garden together.

It turned out that he didn't think gardening was half as much fun as I did. Our afternoons together while I pulled weeds were not the peaceful fun mother-child experiences of my dreams.

I am happiness! I am health! I am wealth!

Fast forward a few decades. My son was now a dad, putting in a garden with my first GRANDchild. Sometimes growing things take longer than you think.

Humans have lived for eons among growing things, intimately connected to plants, animals and Mother Nature. It's only been in the past few generations we've separated ourselves for so much of our lives. I postulate we have created Nature Deficit Disorder.

Think how differently we live from our great grandparents. We live in air conditioned, heated housing, go to work in air conditioned, heated cars and rarely meet Mother Nature without being artificially protected.

Do I want to live the way my great grandmother did? Not on your life! I'm very fond of indoor plumbing. If I want to cook dinner, I'm very happy that I don't have to chop and haul wood to get the fire going.

But, one of the biggest blessings my mother gave me was transferring her love of being outdoors and being active while there. In her nineties, as she was "frailing," she spoke of her enjoyment of being outside while it was snowing, and sweeping off the deck. One of the things she did that enabled her to live 97 plus years was to stay physically active (see Steps 1 & 2).

When we were kids, no matter how busy she was (with nine kids, she was definitely busy!), she'd drop everything when the tide was high and walk to the end of the point with us to swim. I got to "forest bathe," decades before research started to document how beneficial it is to be outdoors in the woods.

I am happiness! I am health! I am wealth!

Grow plants. No longer restricted to the natural growing season, we can grow plants all year, no matter the weather. It's early April as I write; my yard is still snow-covered. No planting today for me.

There are always plants growing in my home. My white geraniums, plucked from my summer garden and residing in front of my south-facing French doors are already blooming. They are surrounded by other plants, plants that clear the air in my home during the months when it's enclosed as tightly as I can make it.

Plants that give off oxygen for me to breathe. Plants that delight my eyes as I tend them and observe them. Plants that enrich my microbiome and thus build my health.

We now know that digging in dirt releases microorganisms, microorganisms that buttress our immune systems. What a gift!

Virtually all of us can bring plants into our living and working environments and will benefit by doing so. Gardening is one of the fastest growing hobbies in the U.S. Vegetables to feed our bodies, flowers to feed our souls.

I am happiness! I am health! I am wealth!

STRATEGIES

1. Purify your air with plants. I recently read that keeping succulents growing in your bedroom increases the oxygen in the air you inhale. Unlike most plants that give off their oxygen during the day, these produce most of their oxygen at night. According to Google, here's a list of them:

    Areca Palm

    Neem Tree

    Snake Plant

    Aloe Vera. One of the most healing plants available.
    I drink Univera aloe every day.

    Gerbera (Orange)

    Christmas Cactus

    Rama Tulsi, Tulsi, Holy Basil

    Peepal Tree

2. In the winter, to assuage your hunger for growing things, stop in to a local greenhouse, just to breathe in that soft moist air and to be around greenery and flowering plants.

3. Buy yourself a plant or flowers for the same reason.

"There are no gardening mistakes, only experiments."

– JANET KILBURN PHILLIPS

STEP #17
Refuse to Be Age-Segregated

A STORY

Last Thanksgiving, I chose to run a 5k on Thanksgiving morning. I had never run a Thanksgiving 5k and I was sure it would be fun. To increase the fun factor, I wore a turkey hat (me, who hates to wear a hat!)

I am happiness! I am health! I am wealth!

There were over 1500 of us who ran that race. Parents with babies in strollers, parents with school age kids running together, seniors (too few women, I'm afraid), a family all decked out in turkey costumes, serious runners, and folks who were walking. All of us running on a crisp Thanksgiving morning, having fun together.

Before and after the race, I talked with people, complete strangers, I'll very likely never see again. They all increased my joy in the day!

I find it very sad to hear older folks express sorrow and loneliness because all their friends have died. I imagine that is excruciatingly painful. For me, that is a very good reason to be friends with folks of all ages.

One of the most awful things we do to seniors is to put them into institutions (bad enough all by itself!) where their only companions (other than staff) is other old people. If the only people I can talk with are those whose life experiences tend to mirror mine, how do I easily access new ideas?

I am happiness! I am health! I am wealth!

I don't. For the past several summers I have worked part-time at a local ropes course. I am surrounded by, and interact with, young, exuberant, competent, enthusiastic, fun young people. They are my work colleagues. Without that job, I would have missed the fun of knowing these kids. They help keep me young. I help them conceptualize that age doesn't need to mean old, that one can be simultaneously vibrantly alive and chronologically "old." Great exchange!

In my networking organizations, Think Local and Social Media Moguls, I regularly interact with people of all ages and nationalities, a great way to bring diversity into my life.

If you have GRANDkids, spend as much time with them as you can. No GRANDS, there are lots of kids who need surrogate grandparents. I'd find it hard to say who benefits most, the kids or grandparents. Who cares? It's a win/win to be in a diverse, age-integrated world. Each generation has so much to offer the other.

Recently, I had spent a Sunday competing in a sprint triathlon with my eldest GRANDdaughter, Charlotte and her friend Alyssa. My older son, Adam, his wife, Liz and second GRANDdaughter, Caroline competed as another team. The age range of the competitors was from nine to 76. What a kick for me; I was the oldest person competing and I had the eleventh fastest swim among the 21 teams! Another kick was being among so many other people of all ages doing something really active. The final kick was playing in a three-generational group of my family.

STRATEGIES

1. Investigate the volunteer opportunities in your community. Love to cook? There are likely soup kitchens in your area who would love your help. My mother and Aunt Barbara volunteered in their local soup kitchen well into their eighties. Love to read? Can the library use your help? What about your local hospital or community garden? Volunteer (or take a paying job) with any organization whose goals or products you love.

2. While you are out in the world, make it a point to interact with as many folks of all ages as possible. Just exchanging smiles is a life-enriching experience for both parties. Are there neighborhood families you can befriend?

STEP #18
Love the Technology

A STORY

As a nurse manager in the early eighties, my hospital set up a computer training program for us. I sat at the key board of the Mac and was paralyzed with fear. I was sure I was going to strike a key and the machine would burst into flame.

I didn't gain much from my introduction to computers; I was too anxious to really pay attention to instructions.

A few years later, I was in graduate school and enrolled in a required research course. One of our assignments was to go the Boston University computer lab and go through a tutorial to get familiar with the equipment.

Even with the help of the teaching assistant assigned to the lab, I could NOT find my way through the password process. After way too many attempts, I gave up and went home.

I am happiness! I am health! I am wealth!

I passed the course, so I must have finally figured out how to log on. Now, I would be absolutely unable to run my life without computers. No one can.

Is it confusing, frustrating, and challenging to learn to use electronic devices? Yes! Those are pretty good reasons to learn and use technology. Challenging our brains to learn to use electronics is great brain exercise. We now know that our brains are neuroplastic, that is, capable of growth through the entirety of our lives. As previously stated, with brains just as with muscles, "Use it or lose it" applies. Learning is necessary for the best expression of our lives.

Technology gives you an enhanced ability to keep learning. I love being able to text the GRANDs as they reach the age where their parents give them the privilege.

Technology enables you to travel without leaving your chair. I find great clips that inspire me and delight me as I peruse Facebook posts. It's also such an efficient way to stay in touch with those I love.

Do I get stressed by technology? I certainly do when it doesn't do what I want it to do as fast as I want it to. For me, it's an opportunity to focus on wanting to not be stressed and choosing to stay relaxed as I deal with it. A good opportunity to ask, "Rita, will this be important in twenty years?"

Technology offers me the opportunity to come up against things I don't know and let not knowing be okay. It's also a great reason to develop connections with younger folks who use technology as if it were second nature, which it is for them.

STRATEGIES

1. Ask questions. I was about thirty when I realized I was expecting myself to know everything! Silly me! I thought about it and realized that it was humanly impossible for anyone to know everything. Whew! Off the hook on that one.

   Then, I learned that if there was something I didn't know and asked, people usually loved my asking.

2. Embrace technology. How I love the coming technology of cars that drive themselves. The "talk" that children have to have with aging parents will be a thing of the past. No longer will parents have their driver's licenses and their independence curtailed because they can no longer drive. Wow! What freedom!

What a lesson in loving technology and not being stressed by it I just gave myself. I had started writing this section, hit the wrong key and lost the data. I took the advice I have been giving and asked: "George (my virtual assistant, George Hamilton, who is such a great resource when my computer is uncooperative), how can I get it back? I know it's somewhere."

(I never did find the lost data and had to re-write it.)

*"The science of today
is the technology of tomorrow."*

– EDWARD TELLER

STEP #19
Don't Sweat the Small Stuff
(It's All Small Stuff)

A STORY

Many years ago, I came across a quote that I loved, "Worry is interest paid on trouble — before it comes due." When I was told I had abnormal cells on a routine Pap smear, I got scheduled for a colposcopy which would enable a closer look at the cells.

When I arrived for the procedure, the doctor commented on my lack of anxiety during the weeks it took to get it scheduled. My observation to him was, "It's either cancerous or not. Why would I spend weeks worrying about something that might be of no concern whatsoever? If I did have cancer, then would be the time to get into action."

I am happiness! I am health! I am wealth!

It was not. My cells were clear of abnormality. I'm very glad I didn't waste any time worrying about it. What we now know is that worrying creates stress. Chronic stress is definitely damaging to our health.

According to pollster Louis Harris, "Fully 90 percent of all adult Americans report experiencing high stress, with as many as six in every 10 reporting "great stress" at least once or twice every week.

Worry, anxiety and stress have a direct impact on our bodies. There is absolutely no doubt about that. Remember the last time you were driving, and looked into the rear view mirror and saw those flashing blue lights. I'll bet you can very quickly describe the changes you experienced in your body. That immediate flood of biochemicals is a life saver when the danger is physical and we need to mobilize our resources quickly to get out of danger.

Our bodies are amazingly well designed to deal with short-term acute stress and completely inept at coping with the majority of the stressors we encounter today, the ones for which a massive physical response is totally ineffective — those ongoing events, where we often don't have time to clear the biochemical leftovers from one event before we are required to cope with three or four additional ones.

In the summer I live in an RV that sits in an absolutely gorgeous spot by the water; I deliberately leave my television at home for several months. Each fall when I return to my home and click on the television, I am always aware of the stress response in my body as I watch the evening news. Once I have grown accustomed to the evening news, I no longer notice the physiological responses I am generating. (Note to self; perhaps you might want to skip the evening news.) Inadvertently by losing my data, I gave myself an experience that is providing the basis for this step.

According to Mark Hyman, MD, stress is implicated in about 95% of the illnesses we are experiencing. Wow! That has profound implications for long-term health, which is the whole point of this book.

A friend used to speak of "grenades that we launch far out into our lives." Unrelieved stress is a big grenade for those of us living the western lifestyle. It is exploding into our lives at unprecedented rates! It is quite literally killing us.

Many years ago, I encountered research done by the Institute of Heart-Math. Research subjects (scientific lingo for people in this case) were asked to imagine something that made them angry for five minutes. Prior to imagining, researchers measured salivary IgA, which is an immune factor found in our saliva. It's our first defense against pathological organisms that enter our bodies through our mouths. (There are a lot of those!)

After the subjects did the five minutes of remembering something that made them angry, the researchers measured salivary IgA again and every hour for six hours. The results were so powerful, that I made a change in my behavior.

The results? Initially, IgA went above the initial reading, but, then fell below baseline and *stayed below baseline for six hours!* My takeaway from that bit of information?

I lived in the greater Boston area and frequently drove on the infamous 128, the site of amazing feats of dangerous driving. Not infrequently, someone would blast by me at high speed, so close the paint on my driver's side door would smoke. (Perhaps I exaggerate here, but only a little).

My immediate, innate reaction would be a flash of fear and anger, often expressed both physically and verbally. After learning about the Heart-Math research, I changed my behavior, by asking, "Rita, is this worth six hours of depressed immune functioning?" The answer was always a re-sounding, "NO!"

The next step was to consciously choose to release the stress reaction, to mitigate the rush of cortisol and adrenalin, to breathe deeply and choose to relax.

The second part of the HeartMath research, done with the same sub-jects, was to have them return to the lab and repeat the same process, only this time to spend five minutes imaging something that they felt good about, experiences that made them happy.

I am happiness! I am health! I am wealth!

This time, salivary IgA initially dropped below baseline, then rose above baseline and *stayed above baseline for six hours!* How lovely to know. Just by thinking happy thoughts, I can vaccinate myself against patho-logical organisms!

As I write this, my country of origin is sprouting more angry thoughts than I can remember. Note to self: protect yourself by observing, stay-ing focused on what you want, which is peace and prosperity, resist the urge to let "them" make me angry, no matter who "them" is.

Another profoundly destructive result of our choosing to live with such unprecedented high levels of stress is that when our adrenals are pro-ducing adrenalin and keeping our bodies in "fight-or-flight or freeze mode," we are not producing DHEA. DHEA is essential for cellular heal-ing and repair.

STRATEGIES

1. Make/take time every day for quiet moments, preferably in an environment where you feel peaceful and relaxed. For my money, you cannot beat spending time outdoors.

2. Develop a meditation habit. There are lots of wonderful audio and video sites on the internet to use as a guide.

3. Exercise!

4. Spend time at the ocean. Live in the Midwest where there hasn't been an ocean in the past couple of million years? Watch the wind ripple though wheat fields where organic wheat is being grown.

5. Find a nearby waterfall and sit beside it, or tune into a waterfall recording.

6. Simply close your eyes and take three or four deep breaths.

"The greatest weapon against stress is our ability to choose one thought over another."

– WILLIAM JAMES

STEP #20
Be the Change
You Want to See in the World

STORY

Several years ago in a Unity prosperity course (Stretton Smith's *4T Prosperity Program — Tithing of Time, Talent and Treasure for Prosperity and the Fullness of Life*), we were told to write 100 times a day, "I am prosperous." Good student that I am and ardently desiring prosperity, I did the exercise faithfully.

I noticed as I did the writing that the word, "prosperity," had no real emotion attached to it. I was writing the words but feeling no energy attached to it. My prosperity did not appreciably increase.

I am happiness! I am health! I am wealth!

In the ensuing years and with much more learning, pondering and introspection, I have come to recognize that thoughts and feelings need to be aligned for our thoughts to be really powerful. I call this being aware of our "themotions;" combining theme and emotion created that word.

When I was dutifully writing "I am prosperous," I wasn't really communicating with the energy of the universe, or whatever name you might choose to call it. Now when I say, "I am prosperous!" I feel the joy of it. I feel gratitude for being prosperous. My themotions are internally consistent.

I like the combination of theme and emotion; to me it expresses the idea that there are themes to our emotions. The belief themes, those ideas we consistently hold in mind, are powerful energies that drive our behaviors, our motions.

Do I want everyone to be prosperous? Absolutely!

The statement that headlines this step, "Be the change you want to see in the world," is attributed to Ghandi, who changed the course of the history of India by his inspired, nonviolent leadership. Underneath the roaring rancor of our current environment, I know that we all want peace, we all want love, we all want health, we all want prosperity.

Science, and virtually all spiritual traditions, tell us that what emerges into our physical reality rises from our perceptions. If I am peace, love, health, and prosperity, I am creating it in the world.

Quantum science and spiritual traditions all teach that the "real world" in which we all live isn't really real at all. It is simply sub atomic particles, flashing in and out of being so rapidly we can't see it happening. That incredibly rapid-fire flashing is the operating system behind my fingers, the energy as I use my mind, totally unconsciously, to consciously have fingers that are tapping on my equally rapidly firing keyboard keys. Amazing!

I am happiness! I am health! I am wealth!

The lesson is: what we focus on is what we experience! For the decade plus that I was so dreadfully ill and incapacitated, I couldn't help focusing on just how awful I felt, thus creating more of feeling dreadful.

As my health declined, so did my bank account. In the U.S., due to the lack of comprehensive definitions of health and well-being, being physically ill is almost always connected to being fiscally ill, too. The stress of being ill is compounded by the stress of being increasingly broke. This is the equivalent of compound interest working against us.

Edwene Gaines (Isn't Gaines a superb name for a woman who teaches prosperity?) gave me the definition of who/what I want to be in the world: prosperity. Her four-part definition:

1) A vibrantly alive physical body

2) Relationships that work all the time

3) Work that doesn't feel like work, but play

4) More money than I can spend.

Don't you love that definition? Wouldn't you love to see that in your life? Would it feel freeing to know that you can create that, no matter what "they" say or do? Wouldn't you LOVE to be that change?

I first encountered that definition several years ago. I was light years away from prosperity then. I spent most of my days on the couch reading fiction (Non-fiction, my preferred mode was too much for my muddled brain to comprehend). Sometimes, my exercise capacity limited me to being unable to walk more than five minutes before I was driven back to the couch.

My relationships weren't working very well either. I didn't have the energy to be a full participant. I still thought, not very consciously (Remember, I was so physically depleted, it was hard for me to think!) that others needed to adjust to my needs.

Most of the time, I couldn't work and nothing felt like play! It takes energy to play.

Money? The early unconscious grounding of my relationship with money was that of passionately wanting more money. The most frequent words I heard were, "We can't afford it." I also got a big dose of the belief system that says "people with money are bad."

Besides which, women of my generation were not expected to generate money or be responsible for their own economic well-being. The worse my physical condition got, the worse my fiscal condition became.

I am happiness! I am health! I am wealth!

Where am I today? Soaring! I am healthier physically, intellectually, emotionally, spiritually and financially than I have ever been in my life! Am I rich? YES and getting richer by the day!

The relationship that has changed the most has been my relationship with me. I have learned to love me, just as I am.

STRATEGIES

1. Select a value you would LOVE to see more of in this world. Peace, for example: the world looks like it could enjoy more peace right now. Develop the habit of noticing what experiences increase the level of peace in your own life. Do more of those activities.

2. Still focused on peace... What do you notice that makes you feel less peaceful? Do fewer of them.

3. Unplug. One of the greatest gifts I give myself every year is the summers in my camper. I DO NOT bring my television with me! I can assure you that it is much easier to feel peaceful with no television input in my brain.

4. Want more prosperity? Figure out ways to help someone else feel prosperous.

5. Get healthier! What steps can you take to get healthier? Do take those steps, even if you can only take one mini-step at a time. In the U.S., with our antiquated ideas and attitudes about healthcare, getting healthier is likely to increase your financial wealth.

6. Smile at strangers. Talk with them. Be actively engaged in conversations and allow the richness of their stories to enrich your life.

I am happiness! I am health! I am wealth!

"A negative mind will never give you a positive life."

– UNITY VILLAGE

STEP #21
Understand That No One Makes You Feel Anything

A STORY

One day, Jim Ritcher said to me, "Rita, you ought to own your own great-ness more than you do." I didn't really get what he was saying to me for the longest time. I had been fed the belief that "Nobody likes a brag-gart." Ever hear, "Don't toot your own horn"? I took that one in, too.

I had learned to believe I was less-than when I was a kid. Internally, I was operating out of those beliefs wherever I went and whatever I did. Grounded in those old, outdated beliefs, I was not allowing myself to achieve what I wanted to achieve.

I am happiness! I am health! I am wealth!

More recently, I stood in the bathroom with my GRANDdaughter, Julia as she was primping and stroking her hair in the mirror and she said, very casually, "I'm admiring myself." Way to go, Jules! May you never stop admiring yourself!

Many years ago, I read a quote from Eleanor Roosevelt. She said, "No one makes you feel inferior without your consent." One of the results of my High Stress/Low Yes childhood and the religious teaching of the hell-fire and brimstone church of my childhood (I was "original sin!") was deep, mostly unconscious, feelings of inferiority to almost everyone!

In self-defense, I developed a pretty good "success face." I was smart and excelled in school. I was a very good athlete (although I certainly didn't really own that). The childhood that forced me into taking care of myself in lots of ways and taking care of younger siblings, along with my native capacities, made me very competent.

But, underneath it all, I did feel inferior. Eleanor's words gave me the insight to decide to change my own opinion of myself. It only makes sense that if I want others to think highly of me, I have to think highly of myself. I have discovered that the more I value and respect myself, the more others do as well.

I am happiness! I am health! I am wealth!

Thinking highly of myself flew directly into the face of all that early socialization. The "nobody likes a braggart" line. The line about "humbling" and "exalting." And that dreadful song they taught me to sing in church, "Oh, Lord, I Am Not Worthy." The teachings, both overt and subtle, about females being second class. That was a lot of stuff to think about and change my feelings around.

Not long after I read Eleanor's words, I added my own twist to it. "In fact, no one makes you feel anything, without your consent. If someone says, "I love you!" and my heart goes aflutter with joy, I am consciously, unconsciously and physiologically consenting to that. Same thing, if someone says with equal passion, "I hate you!"

I can assess if I choose to accept the validity of the other's opinion of me. Real freedom comes from being able to let "them" feel however they feel and know that I can determine my own feelings and choose to be in charge of them. Choosing to be the owner of my own feelings and to decide which ones I will allow to express gives me great freedom to be happy, no matter what "they" choose. I choose to love me with great gratitude and joy! I choose to live healthfully and love my body enough to treat it with the level of care I would extend to a champion thoroughbred horse I owned.

STRATEGIES

1. Every morning when you look into the bathroom mirror, look into your own eyes and say, "I love you!" All to often we have been taught to love others and not ourselves! If you find this activity makes you feel uncomfortable, that means its really important for you to practice.

2. Start a *What I Like About Me* list. Find lots of things to like about you.

3. With GRANDkids, yours or anyone else's, find lots of things to like about them and tell them what you see and value about them.

4. Find things about yourself that you are proud of. Just as it is dishonest to take credit for things you didn't do, isn't it a bit less than honest to not take credit for the good you are?

"No one makes you feel anything without your consent."

– RITA LOSEE

STEP #22
Ask Quality Questions for a Quality Life

A STORY

I learned that one from Tony Robbins decades ago (*Awaken the Giant Within*). He pointed out that most people ask questions along the line of, "How am I ever going to be able to pay my bills?", "Why is my boss such a jerk?", "What did I ever see in him/her?", "Why do I never have enough money?"

That thought really resonated with me; I still remember it vividly after thirty years!

For three plus decades, I had a nerve disorder that was excruciating. The most frequent question I asked: "How can I get this to stop?" Perfectly, logical and reasonable question. Stopping that symptom kept me focusing on the very thing I wanted, desperately, to go away. Remember, what you think about and talk about...?

I am happiness! I am health! I am wealth!

In the last three or four years, I started asking another question, "What can I do to restore every cell in my body to robust health?" Much better question! Much better results!

I saw an ad on television last evening that stated that one-third of Americans don't have any money saved for retirement. Because of my own financial challenges, I can relate!

The question I hear is, "How do I live on a fixed income?" That is a limiting question. For way too long, my questions, spoken and unspoken about money were about "How can I get out of debt?", "Why can I never seem to get this money thing straight?"

My current question: "What is the most fun way I can expand my prosperity?" That question focuses me on "play for pay," an outcome that I do want. As previously mentioned, in the summer I work at a Monkey C Monkey Do, a local ropes course; I play for pay. Am I getting rich on that activity? Monetarily, not yet, but I'm not done here, not by a long shot. All rivers begin with a stream. It is my intention to create rivers of revenue, just for the joy of it.

Am I rich from the experience from working at Monkey C Monkey Do? Oh, yes! In ever so many ways!

Lincoln is quoted (apparently erroneously) as saying, "If I have a tree to chop down, I'm going to spend 55 minutes sharpening the saw and five minutes cutting it down." Carefully sharpening and focusing the questions you ask makes the actual work ever so much easier.

Other fun prosperity questions (remember Edwene's broad definition of prosperity here, please):

- What is the fastest, most fun way I can co-create $1000 (or $10,000)?
- What can I do in the next five minutes to move one of my goals/intentions forward?
- What can I do/think/or say that will increase my energy — or someone else's?
- What would I love? To do right now? To have right now? To give right now?

What's good here?

This question is one I use to teach/coach/cajole myself into asking when I find myself in a "negative" situation. I put it in bold because you can't create positive results from negative energy/thoughts. What your think about and talk about comes about, remember?

For the past couple of weeks, I've been observing myself and other folks around me react to the weather. During the end of March and the beginning of April, we've had a lot of snow, coming after what seems like a long cold winter. We are all eager for spring!

Yesterday afternoon, after a brilliant sunny, but cold, day, clouds moved in and it began to snow heavily. UGH! Not what I wanted!

The impetus of seeing it snow created a wish to create thoughts about what I do want and ask, "What is good here?" Maine farmers have long called April snows, "poor man's fertilizer." This late snow will feed the plants that even now are stirring into life beneath the lingering snow. Also good is the strength of the sun now: this snow will disappear in a flash.

I know that warm weather will return; it always does. I am grateful for that. I am grateful that my house is snug and warm while it snows. I am grateful I got my run in earlier.

On a more significant level, I was forced to spend years as a "couch slouch," a situation not to my liking! By no means was I able to stay focused on what was good about what I was living. There were times when I recognized I was learning to ask for help — a neglected skillset in a Yankee Stoic/Irish Catholic heritage.

I got to practice patience, still not my strong suit. I learned to accept support from others; there were many who gifted me money when I was broke.

I am happiness! I am health! I am wealth!

I was gifted with the works of so many authors; I truly don't know how I would have managed if I hadn't been able to read, especially through those multiple long, long nights when I was unable to sleep.

When I was too sick and didn't have energy enough to cook, my sisters, mother and others made food for me.

Now emerged from the cocoon of my debilitated years, I have a greater appreciation for the gifts of my bounding good health and fitness. My intention is to cell-abrate my good fortune and my good health every day.

My overriding favorite question: *What would I love?*

As I wrote that, I could feel my energy shift into a higher gear, and experience the sensations in my body that accompany feelings of joy and happiness. As I begin the day, asking "What would I love?" opens my energy field to allowing and receiving results I love.

It is with great joy that I conclude this book with my favorite question:

What would you LOVE?

LAST WORDS

I had completed the manuscript for this book — I thought. Then a friend, Duane Contois, made this comment: "If you are retired, you have a job, to take care of yourself!" Wow! That observation is so right on. In this age of ever-escalating health care costs and a move afoot to reduce expenditures, we certainly are well served to hire ourselves to maintain/increase our own health.

My most recent issue of *AARP Bulletin* gives us this horrifying quote: "The average retail price of a prescription drug taken to treat a chronic condition has reached $13,000 a year." (Sept., 2018, Vol. 59, No.7) That's just for ONE chronic condition! What if you have two or three chronic conditions? The bulletin goes on to point out that the $13,000 is "about four-fifths of the average annual Social Security retirement benefit."

But, I digress, although not without purpose. Back to Duane's comment that so hit home with me. As I thought about the word, "job," I thought about the fact that ever so many of us don't want jobs, find them stressful, and feel/felt that our jobs keep/kept us from doing what we love. Maybe, "job" isn't the best word for the concept Duane articulated.

Then, I played around with perhaps we, as seniors, could make taking care of ourselves a hobby. Hobbies are fun, add zest to our lives. But, for me, hobbies connote being a bit too casual about taking care of ourselves. After all, if my hobby is playing solitaire or knitting and I don't feel like playing solitaire or knitting, it's very easy to blow it off and not do it. Not a good idea when it comes to taking care of yourself.

The next was the idea of taking care of ourselves so we can play full-out at the game of life for decades to come. We all like to play, although way too many of us stopped playing a long time ago. Why not decide to play today? Why not decide to play full-out? Why not decide to live in great health, great wealth and great happiness for many decades?

After years and years of having to sit on the sidelines of my own life game, I am now, with great zest and enthusiasm, playing full-out in my life. It is my profound hope that *Soaring Seniors* is a source of inspir-ACTion, for you, that you are so inspired by this material that you take action and play the game of your life — full-out!

RITA RECOMMENDS

BOOKS!

Anthony, William. *Medical Medium: Secrets Behind Chronic and Mystery Illness* and How to Finally Heal. Carlsbad, CA: Hay House, Inc. 2015.

Blum, MD, MPH. *The Immune System Recovery Plan: A Doctor's 4-Step Plan to: Achieve Optimal Health and Feel Your Best, Strengthen Your Immune System, Treat Autoimmune Disease, See Immediate Results.* New York: Scribner. 2013.

Bredesen, MD, Dale. *The End of Alzheimer's: The First Program to Prevent and Reverse Cognitive Decline.* New York: Avery. 2017.

Chatterjee, Dr., Rangan. *How to Make Disease Disappear.* New York: Harper One. 2018.

Cherniske, Stephen. *The DHEA Breakthrough: Look Younger, Live Longer, Feel Better.* New York: Ballantine Books. 1998.

Cherniske, Stephen & Kather, Natalie, MD. *The Metabolic Makeover: It's All About Energy.* Altea Media, LLC. 2014.

Coughlin, Joseph. *The Longevity Economy: Unlocking the World's Fastest-Growing, Most Misunderstood Market.* New York: Hachette Book Group. 2017.

Dispenza, Joe. *Becoming Supernatural: How Common People Are Doing the Uncommon.* Carlsbad, CA: Hay House, Inc. 2017.

Guyenet, PhD, Stephan. *The Hungry Brain: Outsmarting the Instincts that Make Us Overeat.* New York: Flatiron Books. 2017.

Gikandi, David. *A Happy Pocketful of Money: Infinite Wealth and Abundance in the Here and Now.* Charlottesville, VA: 2011.

Hyman, MD, Mark. *Food: What the Heck Should I Eat?* New York: Little Brown and Company. 2018.

Jenkins, JoAnn. *Disrupt Aging: A Bold New Path to Living Your Best Life at Every Age.* New York: Public Affairs. 2018.

Lugavere, Max. *Genius Foods: Become Smarter, Happier, and More Productive While Protecting Your Brain for Life.* New York: Harper Wave. 2018.

Lustig, MD, Robert. *Fat Chance: Beating the Odds Against Sugar, Processed Food, Obesity, and Disease.* New York: A Plume Book. 2012.

Lustig, MD, Robert. *The Hacking of the American Mind: The Science Behind the Corporate Takeover of our Bodies and Brains.* New York: Avery. 2017.

Mctaggart, Lynne. *The Power of Eight: Harnessing the Miraculous Energies of a Small Group to Heal Others, Your Life, and the World.* New York: Atria Books, 2017.

Ortner. Nicholas. *Manifesting Your Greatest Self: 21 Days to Releasing Self-doubt, Cultivating Inner Peace, and Creating a Life You Love.* Carlsbad, CA. 2017.

Perlmutter, David, MD. *Brain Maker: The Power of Gut Microbes to Heal and Protect Your Brain — for Life.* NY: Little Brown and Company. 2015.

Peyton, Sarah. *Your Resonant Self: Guided Meditations and Exercises to Engage Your Brain's Capacity for Healing.* New York: W.W. Norton & Company. 2017.

Smith, Stretton. *4T Prosperity Program — Tithing of Time, Talent and Treasure for Prosperity and the Fullness of Life.* Carmel, CA: 4T Publishing Co. 1998.

Walker, M. *Why We Sleep: Unlocking the Power of Sleep and Dreams.* New York: Scribner, 2017.

Weil, Andrew, MD. *Mind Over Meds: Know When Drugs Are Necessary, When Alternatives Are Better — and When to Let Your Body Heal on Its Own.* New York: Little, Brown and Company, 2017.

Vitale, Joe. *Anything Is Possible: Mind Expanding Secrets for Achieving Y our Biggest, Boldest, Most Bodacious Goals Discovered While Bending Nails, Bolts, Bars, and Horseshoes by Hand!* Wimberley, TX: Hypnotic Marketing. 2018.

WEBSITES!

soaringseniors.com

ewg.org/foodnews

proactivehealthwithanne.com

thehealthyskeptics.com

Telomeres:
ted.com/talks/elizabeth_blackburn_the_science_of_cells_that_never_get_old?inf_contact_key=1f590b02c934d2feac35daad4ae96ea5fcab0b53993 98e00a0d2b9a83b1e9297

SELF-ASSESSMENT WHEELS!

It's common in the U.S. to hear "health, wealth, and happiness." I believe those are written in the wrong order. From my study and introspection of over two decades, it seems a more productive order is happiness, health, wealth. If you are without adequate health, it is extremely unlikely that you will be happy. I can personally attest to the truth of that statement!

If you are without adequate wealth, struggling to make ends meet, that condition also blockades your ability to ability to be happy. In the presentation of these assessment wheels I am reversing the traditional order. Being happy will facilitate the growth of both health and wealth.

"There is preliminary evidence that people who score higher on the well-being scales have better social and work relationships; make more money; live longer, healthier lives; and are more contributory societal citizens." psychologicalscience.org/observer/serious-research-on-happiness

That quote alone is enough evidence for me to expend whatever time and effort it takes to change my life so I boost my happiness quotient.

How to use the wheels

Please duplicate three copies of each, or go to soaringseniors.com and click on "wheels". Once you have your copies, get three pens/pencils of different colors.

Starting with the wheel of your choice and a colored pen, make a dot on each segment that is your best estimate of where you are right now in that category.

Let's use the health wheel as a teaching tool and start with sleep. On average how well are you sleeping right now? The scale runs from one to 10 with zero being dead center (that is a play on words; if you score a zero on any factor, you really are dead for all practical purposes.) My personal estimate is for sleep is a 10, therefore, I'd make a dot on the perimeter of the circle.

Using the same color, make your estimate for each segment. Then join the dots you've made so you have a wheel; obviously, the wider and more circular your wheel, the healthier your health self-rating is.

Once you've created the visual for your current state of health, take a second health wheel and a second color and repeat the entire process, using your estimate of your level of health three years ago. Is your current health estimate better than it was three years ago?

My own estimate of where I was three years ago with regard to sleep is 3 – 4. I often had trouble getting to sleep. More often, I was awake anytime from 1:00 am to 4:00 am and unable to get back to sleep. I chronically got way less than the seven to eight hours of sound sleep we know is necessary for good health.

The last wheel is completed by taking your third copy of the health wheel and the third color. This time, you are estimating what your health will be three years from now, if you make no changes in beliefs or behaviors.

If, after you have completed all three wheels, it is clear to you that you are less healthy today than you were three years ago, the next step to ask is, "If I do nothing to improve my health for the next three years, what will be my state of health *then?*

In three years, you will definitely be three years older, and simply by the passage of time very likely to be less healthy. As I look at my personal health wheel, I have no need or desire to improve my sleep rating. My current rating for stress is around 8; three years ago, it was closer to 4; I can pat myself on my back (and thank Univera for my greatly improved health, which certainly has facilitated a huge reduction in stress). There is, however, room for improvement on my self-rating for further reducing the impact of stress on the quality of my health and well-being.

Repeat the above process with happiness wheel and the wealth wheel. Nothing stays static and unchanging in this universe, so if you want more happiness, health, and wealth in three years than you are enjoying today, I hope this exercise is a spur to inspirACTion. You are inspired *and* you are taking action.

As a senior, it is quite likely that your expectations in all three wheels are expectations of deterioration. Those are old, outdated expectations that do not serve you, those who love you, or the world.

To improve in any segment on any wheel does not require herculean effort; it does require commitment and ongoing actions, day by day. My friend, whom I've never met, James Altucher, taught me that a one percent improvement each day amounts to a 3800 % improvement in a year!

Making that one percent improvement each day is what I have long called mini-steps. What mini-step can you take today to move any of your wheels into a fuller, rounder state? The good news is these categories are not really separated. They all impact other categories: as your sleep improves, your stress level will reduce, your blood sugar will go down, and your relationships will likely improve because you won't be a sleep-deprived grouch.

An aphorism from my childhood resonates: "A rising tide floats all boats."

HAPPINESS WHEEL

HEALTH WHEEL

WEALTH WHEEL

YOUR I-AM-ATHON!

I am initiating this section with a quote from Emmet Fox who said, "We have the key to life and that key is that life is a state of consciousness." Additionally, "The great creative Word is I AM. It is the secret of life." (*Daily Word*, May/June 2018. P 57)

Whatever words we choose to follow, the magic words "I AM" initiate/create our future. I have noticed that as folks age, the answer to the stock question, "How are you?" often elicits a litany of bodily complaints, as in, "I'm so tired, I am discouraged," or "I'm so sick."

When I was so very ill, I fell into that word trap, but stopped it when I learned about "I AM" being my own personal power statement. There are well over seven billion of us on the planet at the moment, but when I say, "I AM," what I am saying applies to me and only me!

I also came to realize that every cell in my body was hearing what I was saying. Not that cells have ears, but on the energy level, words vibrate at different frequencies; our cells, all 75–100 trillion of them, instantaneously feel, and respond to the vibrations of the energy we are putting out. So, please don't tell your cells they are anything but vibrantly healthy and alive.

Since the words that create our futures follow "I AM," it's a good idea to only place positive words after them. For example, when someone asks how I am, I always say, "Terrific!" or "Fantastic!" or "Thriving."

Here is an I-AM-athon for illustration and practice. Like any new habit, only saying positive words will take practice. Initially, if you say, "I am rich," part of you, the conscious part of you who has deep debt and too little income, will say, probably not politely, "Yeah, right!!!" Then tell you all the reasons why you're blowing smoke.

On the physical level, you are broke based on current balances, and saying it will definitely deplete your energy and expectations. From a spiritual perspective, you are a divine, limitless being, and like the Divine, God, Allah, the Big Bang or Uncle Sue, whatever you prefer to call the Eternal Initiator/Creator, you already have all you desire. It may not yet have been converted into physical form, but you live immersed in and surrounded by eternal, limitless abundance.

I-AM-ATHON:

I am so happy and grateful that I am healthy!

I am so happy and grateful that I am happy!

I am so happy and grateful that I am wealthy!

I am so happy and grateful that I am so lucky!

I am so happy and grateful that I am delighted with my life!

I am so happy and grateful that I am strong!

I am so happy and grateful that I am fit!

I am so happy and grateful that I am YOUTH-enating!

I am so happy and grateful that I am capable!

I am so happy and grateful that I am successful!

I am so happy and grateful that I am grateful!

I am so happy and grateful that I am replete with happiness!

I am so happy and grateful that I am amazing!

I am so happy and grateful that I am loving!

I am so happy and grateful that I am loved in all ways, always!

As I did that I-AM-athon, I could feel my energy soaring.

In the radio station of your mind, there is always a broadcast actively running. The Grand Receiver has no option but to send back what it receives. It is our role to broadcast what we desire, in full expectation of receiving.

Your choice: Am I tuned in to WSAD or WJOY?

For me, and I am the only one who gets to choose what I am broadcasting, I much prefer WJOY!

It is with great joy that I am recognizing just how blessed I am. That is my intention and my wish for you as well.

ACKNOWLEDGEMENTS

For too many years, I was a senior who couldn't soar. After years of being a highly trained, highly successful endurance athlete and an accomplished speaker with a national reputation, I found myself with my former life stripped away, my long-term coping mechanisms unavailable, and my once robust bank accounts demolished. During those years, it was almost unimaginable that I could be restored and rejuvenated to the level at which I now live.

Although everyone who has ever been part of my life has made a contribution to the life I now lead and the adventures I now anticipate, there are some individuals who have made extraordinary contributions.

Many years ago, I had the privilege of speaking at a Unity Church in Baton Rouge, Louisiana. After separating from my childhood church, I didn't say the word, "God," for decades unless I dropped a hammer on my toe. The God of my childhood was not a friendly dude. The speaking experience of that first Unity service left me with the thought, "If I ever feel the urge to join a church, it will be Unity. I feel at home here."

A few years later, I found myself living in the only Maine community with a Unity Church; I began attending and gradually found a much friendlier God, a God who was termed "Good Omnipotent." I clearly recall seeing the word, "God" juxtaposed with "good" and thinking, "What an interesting idea!"

Much good and many blessings have stemmed from my Unity community; I am particularly grateful for Rev. Jesse James who served M&Ms at one Easter service and was such a gentle, caring and supportive leader. Also on my Unity gratitude list is Rev. Pat Bessey, Ros Goldsborough, Gail McLean, all the women I participated with as one of the "Kitchen Kweens," and all the folks who attended and participated in classes over the years.

Space precludes naming you all: Please know how deeply grateful I am for your presence/presents in my life. Your love and support lives in the pages of this book.

Yuang Ho Lee, who decades ago discovered the amazing healing properties of aloe ingestion and then sowed the seeds of Univera, the company whose products and science literally gave me my life back. To his son, Bill Lee who owns Univera, Ralph Bietz, the CEO, and all the Univera scientists who have contributed to the wealth of knowledge we now have about the healing properties of plants, I cannot adequately express how grateful I am to you for your leadership, determination, and commitment — and for the products you have brought to market, "the best of nature for humankind" and the world.

Stephen Cherniske gets a standing ovation from me. His brilliance, sense of humor, leadership and commitment to truth and health inspire me. His books provide continual and ongoing learning for me. The work he did as Chief Science Officer of Univera has changed many thousands of people's lives.

To Anne Moreau and Jim Mavor, who came up my walk in April, 2016 when life was at its darkest and gifted me the Perfect Combo®, my introduction to Univera products, a huge thank you! An even huger thank you for ongoing friendship and support.

By early June, 2016, my health was remarkably better, so much so I knew I would tell folks about Univera, and I decided to become an associate. One of the best decisions I ever made. Thanks also to my other business partners, Lisa Ferron, Cheryl and "Loveable Larry" Marquis, Pam Martin, Pat Hill Johnson, Paula Hersom, and to Marie Pelletier, who so graciously hosts our delicious biweekly dinner events.

Thanks to Jeff Ball, whose vision and leadership created Think Local, a Maine business networking group. When I first joined the group, I was not well, but the friendship and kindness of the people in Think Local enabled me to keep a hand in my business life. Currently, many Think Local members are not only business associates but treasured friends.

To all those who gather Down Point on the Fourth of July, I am delighted to be part of that annual tradition and tribute to the bonds of family and friendship. I am delighted that so many, many family members are true friends as well. Nothing in my life would be the same without your love, support, and presence in my life.

Finally, deep love to my sons, Adam and Alden, their wives Liz and Tara and to four fantastic GRANDkids, Charlotte, Caroline, Julia and Evan. As I write this, you range in age from eight to fifteen. It has been joy beyond joy to witness you grow, learn, and become such positive and delightful people. It is my intention to be a Soaring Senior for several more decades so I can be part of, and watch, each of you continue to soar!

"It is never too late to be what you might have been."

– GEORGE ELIOT

Printed in the United States
By Bookmasters